KINGDOM WEALTH CODE

UNLOCK BIBLICAL LAWS FOR LASTING WEALTH
AND KINGDOM IMPACT

DR. JOE TARKON

CONTENTS

Acknowledgements

Nobody writes a book alone. After World War II, as Winston Churchill reflected on how the world rallied to support the United Kingdom, he said with deep gratitude, "Never was so much owed by so many to so few." I feel the same way. This book may have my name on the cover, but it was carried by many hearts and many hands.

In truth, this manuscript began decades ago. From Mary Knoll in Okuku, Ogoja, where I served as editor of the editorial board, to the University of Ife, Ile-Ife, now Obafemi Awolowo University, where I published a campus investigative news magazine, the desire to write and publish has followed me through every season of my life. Yet life kept happening, and the writing never quite made it to daylight until now. This book is the first of many to come. By God's grace, the sermons preached in the City of David, Atlanta, the messages crafted over the years, and the volumes of notes I have scribbled in countless journals will all find their way into print. The next phase of my life is devoted to curating, refining, and releasing them.

There are far too many people to name without surely leaving out someone dear, but a few deserve special mention. My adopted parents, Pastors E.A. and Mrs. Folu Adeboye, I am forever grateful for your presence in my life. My covenant siblings, Emmanuel Ibeshi, Israel Ogbechie, a man with uncanny business sense, and Akin Tella, thank you.

My heartfelt gratitude goes to Dr. Sam Adeyemi, whose counsel and guidance came at just the right time and in just the right way. To Jan Mayen, my editor and writer, you were patient, meticulous, and gracious through every rewrite and every late night change. Thank you.

To my office team, led by Dr. Bola Kushimo, thank you for believing in my literary vision and, together with Doris Bawak and Prince Ifeanyi, for carrying the load of publication behind the scenes. The assistance of Tunde Balogun, my PA, has been invaluable.

And then, my family. They have carried the weight of my schedule more than anyone else. Thank you, Yemi, my wife, for your patience and strength, and for years of reminding me to write "my books." And to my children, Eric, Emmanuel, Adaku, Joel, and MaryAnn, thank you for filling my world with joy and for reminding me of the simplicity and wonder of childhood. I love you all deeply.

This book is dedicated specifically to my late, beautiful mother, Mamkpe Mary, who taught me the fundamentals of entrepreneurship and money management.

To everyone who encouraged, reviewed, prayed, nudged, or simply believed, this book is as much yours as it is mine. Thank you.

INTRODUCTION

My childhood was shaped in Cameroon, where many businesses were owned and run by Nigerians. My parents were no exception. They were entrepreneurs by necessity and by instinct. Over the years they operated different retail ventures, trading in commodities, thrift goods, and agricultural produce, and eventually running a restaurant that sustained us until we left Cameroon.

I watched them navigate slow seasons and long days, negotiation tables and unpredictable markets. I witnessed firsthand the hard work, discipline, and resilience required to make money, as well as the wisdom needed to manage it. My mother, in particular, taught me courage in taking risks and generosity even when resources seemed scarce. She mentored me more through her actions than her words.

By the time I left for boarding school, I was already eager to experiment with small ventures, buying and selling items and spotting opportunities others overlooked. I began with photography in secondary school, then moved into selling books and leather goods, including shoes, bags, and accessories, during university and in the early days of my medical practice.

The entrepreneurial spark my parents ignited has never left me. If anything, it has grown stronger with time. To me, business is not merely about profit. It is about possibility. It is about creating value and making things happen for others. My mind is constantly alive with ideas because opportunities are everywhere.

Formed by the experiences and lessons of my childhood, I am convinced that anyone can learn to make, manage, and multiply money. Not only the wealthy. Not only the naturally gifted. Anyone.

Every believer carries the capacity to walk in Kingdom wealth.

"Beloved, I wish above all things that you may prosper..." 3 John 2

Yet it is one thing to know a promise and another to know how to walk in it. Many sincere and God fearing believers remain limited by a lack of understanding. They know how to pray, fast, and embrace the disciplines of faithful discipleship, yet they have never learned the code, the mindset, principles, and laws that govern financial increase in God's economy.

Kingdom Wealth Code was written to help change that. It will take you on a journey that is practical, spiritual, and deeply personal. It offers fresh perspectives and equips you with timeless principles for financial mastery. Whether you are starting from zero, recovering from losses, or stepping into new levels of influence, this book provides tools to help you move forward with clarity and confidence.

Heaven delights in your prosperity. The world awaits your influence.

"Let them shout for joy and rejoice, who favor my vindication and want what is right for me; let them say continually, 'Let the LORD be magnified, who delights and takes pleasure in the prosperity of His servant.'" Psalm 35:27, Amplified Bible.

I am praying for you. I pray that these pages will awaken in you a calm and certain realization that wealth is not beyond your reach. May God grant you faith, clarity, and confidence to make and manage money effectively for His purpose and glory.

Welcome to the journey.
Welcome to the Kingdom Wealth Code.

Joe Tarkon
Atlanta, Georgia
January 2026

PART 1

KINGDOM FOUNDATIONS FOR WEALTH

1

THE GIFT OF WEALTH

"But remember the Lord your God, for it is He who gives you the power to get wealth, that He may establish His covenant..."
—*Deuteronomy 8:18*

Most Christians admire financial breakthroughs from a distance yet wrestle with guilt the moment they begin to desire it for themselves. Quietly, many equate wealth with worldliness and poverty with holiness, while their homes remain in lack, their dreams unfunded, and their purpose dormant.

This thinking has kept faithful, talented believers poor, not because they lack potential, but because they lack permission. Somewhere along the way, religion taught them to disconnect prosperity from purpose and purpose from provision. The result? An army of kingdom-minded people working with empty hands.

Deuteronomy 8:18 doesn't *suggest* wealth creation; it *authorizes* it. God doesn't just provide; He empowers. He gives strategies, skillsets, divine ideas, and creative insight to produce value and multiply resources. This is not a promise reserved for the elite, it's a covenant right available to every believer willing to align with His principles.

Wealth, in the kingdom context, isn't about luxury; it's about legacy. It's not about accumulation; it's about assignment. The problem isn't money, it's the misunderstanding of its purpose. When believers treat financial abundance as optional or ungodly, they unknowingly limit their ability to serve at scale, build with vision, and leave a lasting impact.

This chapter exposes the myth that wealth is unspiritual. It shows that, according to God's Word, prosperity is a gift wrapped in responsibility. You'll see why wealth is part of your kingdom calling, not something to be feared or avoided but something to be stewarded with boldness and wisdom.

We'll unpack the true meaning of Deuteronomy 8:18 and what it means when God says He gives "power to get wealth." Financial ability is a divine gift, and when used correctly, it activates generational blessing and kingdom expansion.

Let's begin by clearing the fog: wealth isn't a sin and lack isn't a virtue. You were designed by God to create and steward resources for His purpose.

Wealth Is a Gift, not a Sin (Psalm 35:27)

Misguided theology has convinced many believers that poverty is piety and prosperity is proof of compromise. This mindset runs deep, shaping sermons, prayer lives, and financial behavior. For some, the moment money enters the conversation, suspicion follows. The topic becomes taboo, and those who teach it are labeled worldly or materialistic.

Yet Scripture says something very different.

James 1:17 declares, *"Every good and perfect gift is from above, coming down from the Father of lights."* Wealth, like wisdom, peace, or favor, is a good gift. When used according to God's purpose, it becomes a tool of righteousness. It feeds the hungry, funds the mission, frees the oppressed, and builds legacies that outlive the giver.

You must also remember the responsibility that comes with wealth. As 1 Timothy 6:17-18 commands, *"Command those who are rich in this present world not to be arrogant nor to put their hope in wealth… Command them to do good, to be rich in good deeds, and to be generous and willing to share."*

Abraham, the father of faith, was not just blessed spiritually, he was wealthy in livestock, silver, and gold (Genesis 13:2). Solomon asked for wisdom, and God gave him both wisdom and wealth (1 Kings 3:13). Job, after suffering loss, was restored with double his fortune (Job 42:10). These weren't godless men chasing gain; they were covenant people entrusted with resources because of their alignment with God.

Wealth becomes dangerous only when it replaces God, not when it reflects Him. The Bible never condemned wealth, it condemned greed, idolatry, and dishonest gain. Motive is what separates righteous wealth from corrupted riches. As Scripture warns, *"For the love of money is the root of all evil."* (1 Timothy 6:10).

God gives wealth with intention. His provision is tied to His covenant: *"And you shall remember the Lord your God, for it is He who gives you power to get wealth…"* (Deuteronomy 8:18 NKJV). The purpose of prosperity is not personal luxury; it's kingdom expansion. When you see money as a mission tool instead of a status symbol, you stop fearing it and start stewarding it. *"My cities shall again spread out through prosperity,"* says Zechariah 1:17 (NKJV). God is raising financial stalwarts, kingdom treasurers who carry both wisdom and wealth.

In today's world, believers are building schools, launching businesses, funding outreaches, rescuing children, and transforming cities, not just with prayer, but with provision. These are modern-day Abrahams and Esther's, using their influence and income to shape culture and advance the Gospel.

Poverty doesn't glorify God; productivity does. Scarcity doesn't build churches, fund kingdom work, or feed nations. Financial struggle isn't a sign of holiness, faithfulness is. And part of being faithful is managing well what God entrusts into your hands.

Jesus was buried by the generous provision of a wealthy, godly man. *"Now when evening had come, there came a rich man from Arimathea, named Joseph, a disciple of Jesus..."* (Matthew 27:57–60).

Let this truth settle into your spirit: rejecting wealth out of fear or false humility doesn't honor God, it limits your ability to fulfill His call. Wealth isn't a sin. It's a gift that carries responsibility, not shame.

> *To understand why God entrusts wealth to His people, we must look deeper into the covenant promise that authorizes it, Deuteronomy 8:18.*

Understanding Deuteronomy 8:18

Many Christians quote this verse without realizing its weight. It's not casual encouragement; it's a covenant mandate. Deuteronomy 8:18 is not about prosperity alone, it's about divine empowerment for divine assignment.

The first words are a command: *"Remember the Lord your God."* Prosperity can be dangerous without remembrance. When increase arrives and comfort follows, memory often fades. Deuteronomy 8:11-14 warns that forgetting the Lord after abundance leads to downfall.

Wealth creation must stay connected to worship. Success must be anchored in submission. Forgetting the source breeds corruption; remembering the source multiplies blessing with accountability.

God gives you *power* to get wealth, not wealth dropped from the sky but the ability to create it. The Hebrew word *koach* means capacity, vigor, strength. This power is divine enablement, an anointing to create solutions, steward opportunities, and multiply resources through skill, innovation, and wisdom.

Wealth doesn't fall like manna; it flows through relationships, ideas, and execution. The power is given; the results are cultivated. God gave Israel manna for survival but power for production. Manna met hunger; production established legacy.

The reason behind the wealth is covenant. God is not funding luxury; He is fulfilling promise. Abraham was blessed not to boast but to bless nations. That covenant still stands. Wealth without purpose leads to vanity; wealth aligned with covenant builds legacy.

This power is not reserved for pastors or entrepreneurs, it's available to every believer who honors God and applies His principles. Whether teacher, designer, manager, mechanic, or ministry leader, you have access to divine wealth-building grace. The question is not *if* you are qualified, but *if* you are positioned to receive.

You don't need a lottery win or miracle drop; you need clarity, alignment, and activation. The power is in you. The covenant is over you. Now it's time to produce through what God has placed in your hands.

God's Purpose for Prosperity

Money in the wrong hands can destroy, but in righteous hands it builds, heals, and multiplies purpose. God never intended wealth as a status symbol, it is a stewardship assignment.

> Genesis 12:2 says, *"I will bless you… and you shall be a blessing."* Prosperity is not an end goal; it's the fuel for Kingdom impact.

Throughout Scripture, wealth followed responsibility. Solomon received resources to govern, Joseph to preserve nations. The parable of the talents (Matthew 25) teaches that God rewards multiplication, not maintenance. *"Well done, good and faithful servant…"* (Matthew 25:21 NKJV). Prosperity tests trust: *"Whoever can be trusted with very little can also be trusted with much."* (Luke 16:10).

Before abundance, God examines management. Prosperity reveals whether the heart will turn inward or pour outward.

Modern Example: Daniel, a young consultant in Atlanta, tithes from his business profits and mentors entrepreneurs in his church. His financial success became a platform for ministry, not a monument to self.

The call to prosper is the call to stewardship. Genesis 1:28 — *"Be fruitful, multiply, fill the earth, subdue it, and have dominion"*, is God's blueprint for productivity and influence. Prosperity is part of exercising dominion in your sphere.

God's provision always follows His vision. He funds purpose. Kingdom wealth-builders think differently: *How can I use this to solve problems? Whose life will this change?*

A woman in South Africa began selling homemade cleaning products at her kitchen table. Within three years she built a company supplying 100 retailers and employing dozens from her church. She tithes, sponsors missionaries, and funds scholarships. Her increase didn't dilute devotion, it expanded it.

That is the purpose of prosperity: wealth with vision becomes a weapon for impact. It feeds, funds, and frees. It influences policy, empowers the vulnerable, and builds platforms for truth. Broken systems aren't changed by intentions alone but by people who have both the heart *and* the means.

When you see prosperity as a tool, you move from consumer to commissioner. You stop chasing money for comfort and start creating wealth for calling.

Breaking Free from Religious Guilt About Money

Some Christians feel holier when they struggle, as if scarcity proves sanctity. Poverty has been wrapped in religious language and passed down as virtue, but it was never God's truth.

Poverty entered through the Fall (Genesis 3:17-19) and often resulted from disobedience or oppression (Deuteronomy 28:15, 29). Many believers accept lack because they confuse false humility with faithfulness. Real humility doesn't deny what God gives; it stewards it without pride.

Guilt around money doesn't come from God. That shame when you think about increase stems from religious conditioning, not Scripture. God delights in the prosperity of His servant (Psalm 35:27). *"The blessing of the Lord makes one rich, and He adds no sorrow with it."* (Proverbs 10:22).

Romans 12:2 calls for renewed minds, including financial ones. You can't receive what your mindset rejects. Many pray for provision yet feel unworthy when it arrives. Others give generously but resist *receiving* because they fear corruption. This double-mindedness blocks blessing.

Permission to prosper comes from God, not culture. What you have doesn't define you; what you *do* with it does. When your heart is surrendered, wealth becomes a tool for good.

Let shame fall off. Let hesitation break. God has no problem trusting wealth to surrendered hearts. That includes you.

I am not ashamed of prosperity. I receive the power to create wealth for God's glory.

The truth about wealth has been buried under opinion and fear. Scripture restores clarity: wealth is not merely allowed, it is *assigned*. It exists to establish covenant, fund vision, bless others, and expand the Kingdom.

Prosperity is not greed; it's grace with purpose. Abraham, Solomon, Joseph, Lydia, these were not exceptions but examples of covenant stewardship.

Deuteronomy 8:18 is your divine permission slip. God gives you the power to get wealth, and with that power comes the call to multiply, manage, and move in faith. This isn't about chasing riches; it's about answering the call to build with what God has placed in your hands.

You have silenced the voice of guilt that tells you it's safer to stay small. You are not called to shrink, you are called to rise, produce, and reflect the generosity of your Father.

As you move forward, remember you cannot walk in what you're afraid to claim. You have a covenant with the God who gives wealth. Now you're responsible for how you respond to it.

Now that you understand wealth as God's gift, the next step is **knowledge**, because what you don't know about wealth can destroy you. In Chapter 2, we'll uncover the danger of spiritual and financial ignorance and how to overcome it through wisdom, strategy, and truth.

2

OVERCOMING THE BLIND SPOTS THAT LIMIT WEALTH

"If you think education is expensive, try ignorance."
—Derek Bok

Marcus was raised to believe that loving God meant avoiding ambition. His parents warned that too much money could corrupt his soul, so he never asked for more, never learned how money worked, and never pursued anything that looked like wealth. He gave faithfully at church, worked two jobs, and still struggled for decades, frustrated that his life didn't reflect the "abundant life" the Bible described.

Then one day, at a men's conference, he heard a speaker say, *"You cannot rebuke what you've been taught to tolerate."* That statement shook him. For the first time, he realized his poverty wasn't God's test, it was his own ignorance.

This chapter is for every believer who has faith but lacks results; for those who fast, pray, and tithe yet still feel stuck. You may not be lazy or in sin. But if you're unaware of how wealth works in the Kingdom or how money functions in the real world —you will keep spinning your wheels. **Knowledge is the missing piece.**

> *"My people are destroyed for lack of knowledge."* —Hosea 4:6 (NKJV)

Hosea doesn't say people perish for lack of prayer but for lack of knowledge. Destruction isn't always an attack; it can be the result of what you don't know. Many pray for financial breakthrough but remain uninformed about how money is made, multiplied, and managed. The result is bondage, frustration, and cycles of lack.

Ignorance is expensive. It drains potential quietly and keeps even faithful believers struggling. What you don't know can still cost you, financially, emotionally, and spiritually. It leaves you vulnerable to bad decisions and bound to unnecessary struggle.

This chapter will reveal the high cost of staying uninformed. You'll discover why ignorance is one of the greatest enemies of Kingdom prosperity and how real people have broken free simply by learning what they were never taught. You'll see why access to knowledge is one of the greatest weapons against poverty. And you'll be challenged to rise, not just spiritually but mentally, into a new level of understanding.

If you're tired of praying for change but seeing no fruit, this chapter will show you where the gap really is. The truth you don't know can keep you stuck, but the truth you learn and apply will set you free.

My People Perish Hosea 4:6

Some believers are fasting, sowing, and praying in faith while silently wondering why breakthrough seems delayed. They attend every service, quote Scripture, and declare promises, but their finances remain stuck, their ideas stall, and their dreams never launch. The issue is rarely zeal, it's knowledge.

Hosea 4:6 isn't speaking to unbelievers. It says, *"My people."* They are not destroyed by rebellion or laziness but by what they do not know. Destruction follows the absence of wisdom just as disease follows the absence of nutrition.

This reveals a spiritual law: ignorance carries consequences. Not knowing how money works doesn't excuse mismanagement. Not knowing God's view of wealth doesn't shield you from poverty. Whether in finance, health, or relationships, what you don't understand can still cost you everything.

Isaiah 5:13 echoes the warning: *"Therefore My people are gone into captivity, because they have no knowledge."* The enemy doesn't always attack with force; sometimes he attacks with misinformation. *"When people do not know, nor do they understand, they walk about in darkness."* (Psalm 82:5)

There are believers who love Jesus deeply yet live in financial captivity because no one taught them to budget, invest, or monetize their gifts. Others give generously but remain in lack because they were never discipled in stewardship. **Passion without wisdom becomes frustration. Obedience without understanding breeds imbalance.**

The early church devoted itself to teaching (Acts 2:42). Paul filled his letters with doctrine and instruction to equip believers for effective living. Kingdom advancement has always required mental renewal.

God wants you wise, sharp, alert, equipped. You are a Kingdom representative in a world of systems and structures. To operate with impact, you need more than inspiration; you need information. Revelation understood becomes wisdom, and wisdom applied becomes wealth.

Knowledge isn't optional in this season of your life. It's the gateway to strategy, favor, and execution. Don't settle for spiritual survival when God has called you to economic influence. What you're willing to learn determines what God can trust you to manage.

You have permission to grow. You have access to truth. Refuse to remain uninformed while heaven has already made revelation available. You're not here to guess; you're here to govern and it begins with knowledge.

If Hosea warns of the cost of ignorance, the next question is: *What does that cost look like in real life?*

What You Don't Know Can Cost You

A single decision can cost years. One missed opportunity or misunderstood principle can carry massive price tags when truth is absent. The most expensive mistakes are not made from rebellion but from ignorance.

Financial ignorance leads to unnecessary debt, risky investments, and stagnant income. According to the Pew Research Center (2023), individuals with higher financial literacy are far more likely to build lasting wealth. The U.S. Federal Reserve (2023) reports that people without basic financial education are twice as likely to carry monthly credit card balances and pay excessive fees. These outcomes come not from laziness but from lack of knowledge.

Poor health choices often trace back to misinformation or no information. Millions live with preventable conditions simply because no one taught them about nutrition, exercise, or rest. Ignorance in health leaves families grieving and communities burdened.

In relationships, ignorance can be even more destructive. Many endure manipulation or dysfunction because they never learned what healthy love looks like. Boundaries weren't modeled. Emotional awareness was never taught. People settle for toxic patterns not from lack of value but from lack of understanding.

The workplace is no exception. Talented individuals often stay stuck in low-paying roles because they don't know how to negotiate, brand themselves, or pursue growth. Information unlocks access.

Globally, the pattern holds true: where literacy and education rise, poverty falls. The same principle applies spiritually. Quoting Scripture without understanding its systems creates frustration. You can memorize promises yet live in survival mode.

Reflection: What don't you know that's costing you? Is it financial systems, communication skills, or business development? Whatever the gap, fill it. Find a mentor. Read a book. Pay for the course. *Go where the information flows.*

Ignorance has robbed enough people of peace and progress. Information is an investment; what you don't know costs more than what you fear to learn. Once you choose wisdom, the return is unlimited.

Knowledge as a Tool of Liberation

"Through knowledge shall the righteous be delivered." —Proverbs 11:9

Chains don't always rattle. Some appear as fear of success, confusion, or hesitation. They remain locked until truth enters. You can pray for freedom and fast for breakthrough, but without knowledge the door stays closed.

"You shall know the truth, and the truth shall make you free." —John 8:32

Freedom begins with wisdom. Knowledge opens the mind before it multiplies the bank account. Ignorance keeps believers boxed in while information moves others into dominion. The same Kingdom belongs to both; the difference is understanding.

Nelson Mandela said, *"Education is the most powerful weapon which you can use to change the world."* Ignorance is not neutral; it robs and deceives. Education: biblical, practical, applied, breaks strongholds.

C. S. Lewis warned through *The Screwtape Letters* that the enemy's strategy is to keep people from discernment and learning.

Robert Kiyosaki taught that poverty is not a paycheck problem but a knowledge gap: *what you understand, you can control; what you don't understand controls you.*

Pastor E. A. Adeboye, General Overseer of the Redeemed Christian Church of God, a mathematician and a man with great insight, believes good success is built on knowledge and wisdom: *"In all your getting, get understanding."* Proverbs 4:7

Janice, a 52-year-old mother of three, lived paycheck to paycheck until she attended a financial-literacy workshop at her church. Learning to budget, build credit, and invest small amounts changed her life. Within three years she cleared her debts and began saving for her children's education. Her income didn't triple overnight but her knowledge did, and that changed everything.

You are one decision away from a new financial future. The difference between survival and stewardship is knowledge, and between knowledge and results is action. God's wisdom is not a substitute for learning, it is an invitation to pursue it.

Knowledge doesn't just break chains; it builds bridges. What you learn today can deliver you from years of frustration tomorrow.

Three things you can learn this year that will set you free financially:

- **Budgeting:** assign every dollar a purpose.

- **Negotiation:** advocate for your value in business and career.

- **Investing Basics:** understand compound interest and passive income.

These are not luxuries; they are weapons in the hands of the wise.

The Link Between Ignorance and Poverty

"Fools die for lack of understanding." —Proverbs 10:21

Poverty often hides behind tradition or religious phrases. But beneath the surface, ignorance not virtue, fuels most long-term struggle. *"Poverty and shame shall be to him that refuseth instruction."* (Proverbs 13:18) Refusing to learn doesn't just leave you uninformed; it leaves you broke.

In many families, learning stops when school ends. Growth is seen as optional, comfort prioritized over change. Without realizing it, people pass down the mindset: *"This is just how life is."* But life is shaped not by what you inherit, but by what you learn beyond it.

The poverty mindset assumes increase is for others. Ignorance goes further, it lacks the tools to question its own limits. According to UNESCO (2017), nations with low literacy suffer higher poverty. The Harvard Opportunity Insights Project (2018) found that exposure to quality education dramatically increases lifetime earnings. Education opens access, knowledge breaks ceilings.

Take something as simple as tax law: most people overpay because they never learned deductions. Real estate, marketing, and technology follow the same rule those who learn lead. The world doesn't withhold opportunity; it rewards preparation.

If poverty runs in your family, don't just rebuke it, *research it.* Every time you grow in wisdom, you change what your children inherit. That's not just deliverance; it's legacy.

You are not poor; you are under-informed. That's not shame; it's revelation and invitation. God's Word calls you to rule and reign, but rulership requires wisdom. Access is no longer the problem; commitment to learning is. Every excuse that keeps you from growth must die. This isn't hustle culture, it's obedience. *"Take firm hold of instruction... for she is your life."* (Proverbs 4:13)

Knowledge is leverage. You don't have to repeat what your parents didn't know. Poverty breaks when truth enters and now you hold the key.

Ignorance isn't harmless; it's costly. Every delay in learning adds weight to chains meant to be broken. The enemy doesn't always need to lie, he just needs you unaware.

Information is not optional in the Kingdom; it's a tool of freedom. Each truth you pursue adds another key to your purpose. What you learn next can change everything. Every step toward knowledge is a step toward your calling.

Reflection: Pause for a moment. What truth have you avoided learning because of fear or pride? What investment in knowledge have you postponed? Decide today to act on what you know and pursue what you don't.

Now that you understand the high cost of ignorance, it's time to discover the wealth covenant that God made with our spiritual forefathers and how you're connected to it today. This covenant isn't theory; it's a legal, spiritual agreement that carries power, promise, and provision for those who walk in it.

Chapter 3 will reveal why wealth is not only permitted by God but also protected and perpetuated through covenant. You'll see how Abraham's blessing wasn't just historical, it's personal.

You don't have to chase wealth when you understand you're already positioned to receive it. Let's explore how.

3

The Covenant Blueprint for Wealth

"God's covenant with Abraham is not just history, it's your spiritual DNA."

What if your wealth isn't a dream but your birthright?

What if God already made provision for your prosperity, not through a modern financial trend, but through a covenant that predates your existence and extends beyond your lifetime?

Most believers associate wealth with effort or luck, but Kingdom wealth isn't rooted in hustle; it's rooted in inheritance. Long before you were born, God established a covenant with Abraham. It wasn't just about land and descendants, it was about access, influence, and provision with purpose. Through Jesus, that covenant became your legal right.

Galatians 3:29 declares, *"If you belong to Christ, then you are Abraham's seed, and heirs according to the promise."*

This is more than theology; it's a transfer of ownership. When you came into Christ, you didn't just receive salvation, you were connected to a generational promise of divine blessing and abundance.

This chapter reveals the foundation of Kingdom wealth. You'll see how God's original promise to Abraham didn't stop with him, it expanded through Isaac, multiplied through Jacob, and now flows through every believer connected to Jesus. You'll also learn what that inheritance includes, how it functions, and what kind of responsibility it carries.

Covenant wealth isn't passive; it carries accountability. You don't receive it to indulge in luxury, you steward it to build, bless, and expand God's influence on the earth. It's not about what you can consume, but what you've been assigned to distribute.

If Chapter 2 exposed the danger of ignorance, this chapter reveals the power of identity. You're not asking for permission to prosper; you're being invited to step into covenant and activate what already belongs to you.

The Abrahamic Covenant

God never builds anything lasting without first establishing covenant. When He chose Abraham, He initiated more than a promise; He created a divine contract designed to outlive one man and transform nations. That covenant is not ancient history, it's the legal foundation of wealth for every believer in Christ.

In Genesis 12:1–3, God calls Abraham to leave what is familiar and step into a new dimension of obedience. In exchange, God gives a sevenfold promise: to make him a great nation, bless him, make his name great, make him a blessing, bless those who bless him, curse those who curse him, and cause all families of the earth to be blessed through him. Embedded in that promise is Heaven's economy, blessing for the sake of impact.

> Genesis 13:2 records the result: *"And Abram was very rich in cattle, in silver, and in gold."*

His wealth was not accidental, it was covenantal. God resourced Abraham with ownership, influence, and mobility because Abraham was assigned to build legacy and represent Heaven on earth.

Wealth was never the goal; it was the tool. Abraham sought God, not gold. Because of that pursuit, God trusted him with both spiritual authority and tangible abundance. Genesis 17:7 calls it an *"everlasting covenant"*, one that still operates today.

The covenant included **land** (ownership and territory), **fruitfulness** (increase and productivity), and **blessing** (divine favor and protection). These three form the foundation of God's economic system.

The New Testament confirms that this covenant didn't end, it expanded.

Galatians 3:13–14 teaches that *"Christ redeemed us from the curse of the law... so that the blessing of Abraham might come to the Gentiles through Christ Jesus."*

This means the same covenant that enriched Abraham now empowers you.

Jesus came not only to save souls but to reconnect His people to divine inheritance. Galatians 3:29 seals it: if you belong to Christ, you are Abraham's seed and heir according to the promise. Heirs don't earn, they inherit.

You're not reaching for blessing; you're positioned inside it. The covenant that started with Abraham runs through the cross and into your life right now. You're not striving to qualify; you already qualify through Christ's finished work.

Reject the lie that wealth is ungodly. Abraham was righteous and wealthy. He was known in heaven and respected on earth (Genesis 21:22). His prosperity didn't corrupt him; it confirmed his covenant alignment. The same is true for you.

You are not starting from zero. You operate under a blessing older than your bloodline and stronger than any economy. The covenant that made Abraham influential can do the same through you, if you believe it, receive it, and steward it.

Generational Wealth in the Bible: Abraham, Isaac, Jacob

Covenant wealth was never meant to stop with one person. When God blessed Abraham, He was thinking generationally.

Genesis 26:12–14 shows that *Isaac sowed in famine and reaped a hundredfold.* His wealth wasn't random, it was a continuation of Abraham's blessing.

Isaac didn't inherit money; he inherited a **mandate.** Physical assets can be lost, but a covenant blessing multiplies across time and territory.

Jacob built on that foundation. In Genesis 30:43, he became "exceedingly prosperous," using divine strategy revealed in a dream. What looked like dependence turned into dominion. The covenant created transfer, favor that outgrew his environment.

Joseph extended that legacy to national impact. Through divine wisdom, he managed Egypt's economy during famine, saving nations. Covenant wealth doesn't depend on conditions, it responds to obedience and revelation.

Modern examples confirm the pattern. Families like the Rockefellers and Waltons demonstrate how disciplined systems preserve wealth across generations (Forbes, 2023; CNBC, 2021). But Kingdom wealth operates on a **higher covenant.** It's sustained not merely by trusts or offices, but by alignment with God's principles.

Jesus reaffirmed this in John 10:10, He came that you might have life "more abundantly."

> 2 Corinthians 8:9 reminds us that *"though He was rich, yet for your sakes He became poor, that you through His poverty might become rich."*

This is divine exchange: He emptied Himself so you could be filled.

This abundance isn't meant to terminate on you, it's meant to flow through you. How you manage wealth matters. What you teach your children matters. Every generation is meant to inherit both revelation and resources.

Reflection: What financial or spiritual legacy are you building for those who come after you? Are you transferring struggle or strategy, fear, or faith?

The covenant wasn't situational, it was perpetual. It worked in famine, captivity, and foreign lands. It still works now. You're part of that lineage. God blesses in generations, and your stewardship determines how long that blessing stays in motion.

Why God Blesses His Children with Wealth

Wealth is not God's reward for goodness; it's His tool for advancing purpose.

Zechariah 1:17 declares, *"My cities shall again spread out through prosperity."*

When God blesses His people financially, He's not responding to greed, He's resourcing mission. Prosperity funds purpose.

In Genesis 12:2, God tells Abraham, *"I will bless you... and you shall be a blessing."* That phrase defines Kingdom economics. The blessing was never meant to stop with you. When God places wealth in your hands, He is trusting you to build legacy, uplift others, and expand His influence.

From the tabernacle in the wilderness to the early church, every divine assignment required provision. Today's ministries, schools, and humanitarian works stand on the same principle. Organizations such as Convoy of Hope, Africa Missions

Global, and World Vision demonstrate how **wealth with purpose** becomes **impact at scale.**

As Ayn Rand observed, "Money is only a tool. It will take you wherever you wish, but it will not replace you as the driver" (*Atlas Shrugged*, 1957).

Wealth amplifies direction. When your heart is right, money becomes a vessel of righteousness.

Wealth in the hands of the righteous breaks cycles of poverty. It restores dignity, funds education, and fuels transformation. Poverty doesn't glorify God; productivity does. God blesses His people so that His vision can move forward on earth.

Reflection: If God multiplied your income tomorrow, what Kingdom purpose would you fund first?

Increase is a test; will you manage it for mission or merely for comfort?

Covenant Responsibility: Wealth for Purpose, Not Pleasure

The covenant grants access; character guarantees longevity. God doesn't give wealth simply as a reward for faith but as an assignment that demands stewardship, wisdom, and discipline.

In Matthew 25, the Parable of the Talents reveals this truth. The faithful servants multiplied what they were given and were rewarded. The one who buried his gift lost everything. Increase is a **mandate**, not a bonus.

Luke 12:48 declares, *"To whom much is given, much will be required."*

When God increases you, He expands your influence and your responsibility. More isn't about luxury, it's about leadership.

Covenant responsibility means handling wealth strategically, budgeting, investing, giving, and saving with purpose. Multiplication is expected, not optional. Value creation, through business, innovation, or service, is the natural outcome of covenant thinking.

Reflection: Are you managing wealth emotionally or strategically? Where might God be asking you to build structure before sending more?

Money reveals character. 1 Timothy 6:10 warns that "the love of money is the root of all kinds of evil." God never condemned wealth; He condemned idolatry. Money is a servant, not a master.

You are called to be a steward, not a consumer. Financial maturity is spiritual maturity in motion. That means learning, planning, and submitting your goals to God.

The covenant brings blessing, but it also brings weight. When you carry wealth, you carry assignment. You are building what Heaven can trust and Earth can benefit from.

Wealth without purpose becomes waste. But wealth with clarity becomes legacy.

Covenant gives access; character preserves it.

You are not praying for wealth; you are positioned in it.

You're not begging for increase; you're authorized to multiply.

What began with Abraham continues through you because of Christ. This covenant wasn't built for short-term comfort but for generational impact. God is raising builders, not hoarders. If He has trusted you with the blessing, He expects you to multiply it with wisdom and integrity. Before you can walk fully in the wealth God has promised, you must **think like someone who has already received it.**

Your mindset is the vault that either locks or releases the blessing. The next chapter will reprogram that mindset, aligning your thoughts with Kingdom abundance so you can manage what Heaven entrusts to your hands.

4

Transforming Your Mindset for Increase

"Keep your heart with all diligence, for out of it spring the issues of life." —Proverbs 4:23 (NKJV)

Two people can grow up in the same home, attend the same church, and pray the same prayers, yet live completely different financial lives. One builds a thriving business. The other stays stuck in survival. The difference isn't God or opportunity. The difference is mindset.

Thoughts shape outcomes. Beliefs create ceilings. Financial breakthrough starts in the mind before it ever shows up in a bank account. What you believe about God, yourself, money, and purpose will either limit you or launch you. Your mindset is either a gate or a wall.

Romans 12:2 calls us to be "transformed by the renewing of your mind." Transformation is not instant; it is intentional. Every principle in this book rests on this foundation. God can declare increase, but if your thinking is shaped by fear or lack, you will live below covenant level.

This chapter helps you understand how your mind affects wealth. You will learn how mindsets form, through family, faith, trauma, and repeated language, and how to replace limiting beliefs with Kingdom truth. You will also get practical tools: declarations, Bible meditation, and daily habits that train your mind to expect abundance, not shortage.

If you want to walk in wealth, start with wisdom. Transformation begins in your mind. Until your mindset changes, your money patterns will not.

Romans 12:2 Transformation by Mind Renewal

You can love God and still live trapped by old thought patterns. You can be filled with the Spirit and still think from a place of fear, scarcity, or unworthiness. Romans 12:2 is clear: you must renew your mind to experience real change.

Paul wrote this to believers, not unbelievers, showing that salvation and mental renewal are two different processes. Salvation brings new life. Renewal brings new thinking. Until your thoughts agree with God, you will live beneath what He promised.

Your thoughts empower your destiny or delay it. You can pray for provision but sabotage it with unbelief. You can sow seed yet cancel your own harvest through fear. Matthew 8:13 says, "As you have believed, so let it be done for you." Belief sets the boundaries of your life.

Your view of God matters. If you think He only wants to bless you spiritually, you will hesitate to pray bold prayers for increase. If you think you're unworthy, you will reject opportunities He sends. Renewal confronts these lies and replaces them with truth.

Every adult carry belief formed in childhood. Some were taught "money is evil," "wealth is prideful," or "rich people are greedy." Others learned to glorify struggle as holiness. These beliefs become subconscious rules that limit your financial life until you challenge them.

Mind renewal is your responsibility. It requires daily exposure to truth. First Timothy 4:15 says, "Meditate on these things... that your progress may be evident to all." One verse won't undo years of conditioning, but consistent truth will rewire how you think.

Start with declarations. Speak life over your finances and purpose:

- "I am a wise steward."

- "God gives me power to create wealth."

- "I walk in clarity and abundance."

Journal the lies you've believed and confront them with scripture. Replace them with passages like Deuteronomy 8:18 and 1 Timothy 6:17. Let the Word become your mental framework.

Also guard what you consume. The voices around you shape your thinking. Surround yourself with mentors and messages that reinforce faith, not fear.

A renewed mind sees money as a tool, not a threat, and opportunity as assignment, not danger. The more your mind aligns with God's truth, the more you will move in confidence, strategy, and Kingdom authority.

Wealth begins where mindsets shift.

Destroying the Poverty Mentality

You can give, pray, and worship, and still live with a poverty mindset. This mindset accepts struggle as normal, views wealth with suspicion, and treats survival as spirituality. It hides behind phrases like "I don't need much" or "I just want enough." It makes lack feel noble and abundance feel dangerous.

A poverty mindset is rooted in fear, unworthiness, and scarcity. It whispers that success is for others, that wanting more is selfish, and that increase will corrupt you. This mindset leads people to settle, self-sabotage, and resent those who prosper.

Signs of a poverty mindset include:

- Expecting shortage

- Feeling guilty for success

- Making decisions from fear instead of vision

- Settling for less

- Resenting others who grow

But the Bible presents a different picture. God is not poor. Heaven is not broke. Scripture shows God delights in the prosperity of His people (Psalm 35:27). Scarcity is not humility. Lack is not holiness. Poverty limits purpose, generosity, and Kingdom impact.

Financial leaders like Dave Ramsey and Tony Robbins explain that poverty thinking causes people to play small, avoid risk, and delay building anything lasting, not because of money, but because of mindset.

History shows that when nations shift their mindset, everything changes. Japan, South Korea, and others rose from devastation to global leadership, starting with belief, not funding.

The same is true individually. "As a man thinks in his heart, so is he" (Proverbs 23:7). Your thoughts shape your future. When you think Kingdom, you attract strategy, creativity, and favor.

To break poverty thinking, identify the beliefs holding you back. Who told you wealth was wrong? Who taught you to fear increase? Replace those lies with scripture. Write new declarations. Surround yourself with mentors who think bigger. Exposure expands possibility.

Your mindset is a thermostat. If you want new results, raise your thinking. You were designed for abundance and equipped for stewardship.

Proverbs 23:7 You Are What You Think

What you believe about yourself shapes what you expect from life. Proverbs 23:7 says, "As a man thinks in his heart, so is he." This isn't just spiritual truth, it affects how you see money, opportunity, and your ability to create change.

Identity drives behavior. If you believe God made you capable and assigned you purpose, you will move with confidence. But if you see yourself as unworthy, powerless, or always behind, you'll shrink in every opportunity that demands leadership.

Many people pray like heirs but think like beggars. They confess abundance but make decisions from fear. They give from pressure instead of purpose. Until your identity changes, your finances won't.

God calls you a royal priesthood (1 Peter 2:9). Royalty doesn't beg. Priests don't panic. You are designed to lead, build, and steward resources with strength. Your expectations should match your calling.

You are not a burden; you are a solution carrier. God placed gifts in you that solve problems and create value. Wealth is not who you are, but you *are* someone God can trust with increase.

Try this simple reset:

Activity: Write down 3 limiting beliefs you've believed about money.

Now replace each with scripture-based truth:

- "I never have enough" → "My God supplies all my needs." (Philippians 4:19)

- "I'm not good with money" → "I have the mind of Christ." (1 Corinthians 2:16)

- "I'm always behind" → "The Lord is my Shepherd. I lack nothing." (Psalm 23:1)

Speak these daily until they become your new default.

Your words shape your thoughts.

Your thoughts shape your future.

Identity leads income. Think like a steward. Think like a builder. Think like a child of the King.

Think and Grow in God

Napoleon Hill taught the world to "Think and Grow Rich." But Kingdom wealth works differently. You don't just think and grow rich, you Think and Grow in God.

Worldly success relies on ambition alone. Kingdom success flows from alignment:

renewed mind + faith + obedience = supernatural results.

You grow in God by letting Him shape your thoughts, guide your desires, and lead your decisions. Proverbs 3:5–6 teaches us not to lean on our own understanding but to trust Him, submit to Him, and let Him direct our paths.

A renewed mind doesn't just think big. It thinks right. It thinks with God's wisdom. Wealth without direction becomes a trap, but wealth guided by God becomes purpose.

Growth in God means pursuing excellence, discipline, and integrity, not hype, shortcuts, or emotional decisions. It means letting God refine your motives so your goals serve His will, not ego.

When your thoughts align with God's truth:

• You grow with clarity

• You build with wisdom

• You prosper with purpose

• You rise without compromise

Success becomes a fruit of alignment, not striving.

Thinking and growing in God requires intentionality:

Read the Word daily.

Pray for wisdom.

Invite God into your plans.

Let Him reshape what you believe is possible.

Goodness and mercy don't follow you by accident. They follow you because your thoughts and steps align with God's path.

How to Break Mental Strongholds

Strongholds don't live in your environment; they live in your mind. You can change jobs, churches, or cities and still feel stuck if your thinking hasn't changed.

Second Corinthians 10:4–5 says our weapons are mighty through God to pull down strongholds and bring every thought into obedience to Christ.

Strongholds are not small habits. They are entrenched lies that fight truth.

Common financial strongholds include:

• Fear of failure

• Generational programming

• False humility

• Fear of success

• Mental ceilings created by upbringing or past loss

These lies convince you to play small, avoid opportunity, or reject increase.

You break strongholds with:

1. Truth

Scripture is the wrecking ball that shatters lies.

Speak it.

Write it.

Repeat it.

Let it build new mental paths.

2. Exposure

Get around people who think higher.

Learn from books that stretch your vision.

Watch testimonies that make increase feel normal.

Exposure destroys limitation.

3. Mentorship

God uses people to pull you out of patterns you can't see.

The right mentor reveals blind spots, challenges your thinking, and helps you grow with strategy.

4. Consistency

Your brain can be rewired.

Neuroscience confirms what scripture taught first:

Truth + repetition = transformation.

Strongholds are not permanent.

You are not stuck.

You are being transformed one thought at a time.

Daily Mind Renewal Practices

Transformation is not a moment, it's a lifestyle. Here are simple daily tools for renewing your mind:

1. Morning Declarations

Your first words shape your day.

Declare:

- "I am a steward of divine wealth."

- "God gives me power to create value."

- "Wisdom and favor lead me."

• "Resources flow to me for Kingdom purpose."

Say them boldly. Tone and repetition train your mind.

2. Scripture Meditation

Choose 1–2 verses each week to meditate on:

Deuteronomy 8:18

Proverbs 10:22

Romans 12:2

3 John 2

Ask yourself:

"What is God telling me about identity, abundance, and stewardship?"

Write the insights down.

3. Vision Board

Create a vision board that reflects your calling, goals, and Kingdom assignments.

Make it visible. Make it prophetic.

4. Accountability + Mentors

Find someone already walking in the mindset you want.

Share goals and habits.

Let them challenge you with love and truth.

Growth accelerates with partnership.

Your financial future starts in your thoughts, not your wallet. Transformation doesn't begin with hustle or striving; it begins with a renewed mind. Romans 12:2 isn't just a suggestion; it's the blueprint for lasting change and the key to every blessing God wants to release. If your mindset doesn't shift, your money habits won't either. God wants more for you, but your thinking must rise to meet what He's already declared.

You were never designed to live with a poverty mentality. That mindset must be uprooted and replaced with truth. You are what you think, and the Word makes it clear,

God sees you as equipped, worthy, and capable of stewarding abundance. Mental strongholds don't have to rule you. They can be cast down, rebuilt, and reprogrammed by the truth of God's Word.

This process is daily. One verse won't fix a lifetime of fear, but intentional renewal will. Use the tools, declare the truth, and walk out the mind of Christ with purpose. Strongholds must be torn down. The truth can rebuild your life in alignment with God's will, stronger and richer.

Use the tools.

Speak the truth.

Renew your mind daily.

> **You're about to think, and live, at a new level.**

5

God's Economic Framework

"Money is not the root of all evil, the love of money is." – 1 Timothy 6:10 (paraphrased)

If wealth is dangerous, why are Heaven's streets paved with gold? Why doesn't the devil simply use money to destroy every believer? Those questions expose a common myth: that God prefers your poverty over your prosperity.

Many Christians inherited a belief that riches and righteousness cannot live together. But from Genesis to Revelation, God blesses His people with resources and expects them to use them for influence and impact.

God doesn't hate wealth. He hates idolatry. Wealth becomes a problem only when it replaces Him. The belief that "a rich Christian is a compromised Christian" has kept many believers stuck, praying for provision while fearing prosperity. You can't receive what you secretly distrust. Double-mindedness blocks increase.

Heaven sees wealth through covenant, generosity, and assignment. God owns everything. When He blesses you, it's not only for comfort, but also for purpose.

This chapter will help you see money the way God does, without guilt, fear, or confusion. You will see how Kingdom abundance differs from worldly greed, and how God used wealthy people like Abraham, Joseph, and Lydia to advance His plan.

You are about to see money from God's side of the table. When you do, everything changes.

God's Abundance vs Worldly Excess

Many believers confuse abundance with excess. Some avoid wealth, fearing pride. Others chase wealth, thinking it proves God's favor. Both extremes miss God's heart.

Jesus spoke openly about abundance. John 10:10 says He came to give life "more abundantly." Psalm 23 declares, "I shall not want." Ephesians 3:20 says God can do "exceedingly, abundantly" more than we imagine. Heaven's language is not small, it is generous.

The problem is not abundance. The problem is misaligned abundance.

The world pursues wealth for status, control, and image. The Kingdom gives wealth for stewardship, generosity, and purpose.

Here is the clear difference:

Kingdom wealth comes with assignment. Abraham was blessed to be a blessing. Joseph managed a nation through crisis. Solomon's resources built the Temple. Their wealth moved God's plan forward.

You don't need to fear nice things. God is not offended by blessing; He is offended when blessing becomes a god. When wealth serves purpose, it becomes a tool.

Contentment is a major difference. Kingdom abundance brings peace. Worldly excess brings pressure. One is steady. The other is restless.

You're not called to chase wealth the world's way. You're called to build, steward, give, and multiply. When God guides your increase, your wealth becomes a weapon for good.

Let this truth settle:

Earthly wealth is measured by what you keep.

Kingdom wealth is measured by what you give.

The Role of the Believer in the Marketplace

The marketplace is not neutral. It is a battleground for influence. Culture is shaped there. Values are tested there. Lives are impacted there.

Many believers limit "ministry" to church buildings. But God's plan includes boardrooms, studios, classrooms, courts, and tech labs. The marketplace is a mission field.

Jesus said, "You are the light of the world." Light enters dark places. It reveals truth. You are called to influence, not hide.

The Kingdom assignment is not limited to Sunday. It's meant to infiltrate Monday through Saturday. God wants His people positioned in business, media, politics, education, and technology, not to blend in, but to stand out. Every industry needs light. Every system needs integrity. Every culture needs truth that is lived, not just preached.

Daniel served pagan kings and shaped national policy. Joseph led Egypt's economy and saved nations. The Proverbs 31 woman excelled in business, real estate, leadership, and family.

These weren't "secular" jobs. They were Kingdom assignments.

Today, leaders like David Green (Hobby Lobby), Tim Tebow, and Kathie Lee Gifford carry faith into culture. Their work preaches louder than a sermon.

You preach through:

- excellence

- integrity

- generosity

- skill

- leadership

- consistency

Your job is not "secular." Your business is holy. Your work is worship.

God is raising a generation that knows how to carry anointing into every sphere of society. Your platform doesn't have to be famous to be effective. Your consistency, your strategy, your solutions, they all speak. The world doesn't need more hype. It needs hope. And hope flows through believers who take their marketplace call seriously.

Stop waiting for a pulpit. **Your platform is your pulpit.**

When you see your career through Heaven's eyes, you stop chasing opportunity and start carrying authority.

God will use your career, your business, your skills, and your network to reveal His glory. But it starts with ownership. Stop separating sacred and secular. In the Kingdom, everything is sacred when it's surrendered. That meeting, that product, that email, it matters.

So, work like it's worship. Build like it is a ministry. Lead like it is a legacy. You are not just clocking in for a paycheck. You are sent. You are planted. You are called.

Your business is holy. Your creativity is a weapon. Your influence is a ministry. Every client you serve, every deal you make, every classroom you lead, every solution you build, these are not just tasks. They are touchpoints of Kingdom expansion.

And when you see your marketplace role through Heaven's eyes, you won't chase opportunity, you'll carry authority. The world is waiting for believers who do more than speak truth. It's waiting for those who *live* it, with courage, strategy, and excellence. Let that be you.

Prosperity with Purpose

Money without mission is noise. But when tied to purpose, it becomes power.

Deuteronomy 8:18 says God gives wealth "to establish His covenant." Wealth funds Kingdom work. It fuels assignments.

Second Corinthians 9:8 says God gives abundance so His people can "abound in every good work."

God is not moved by greed, but by purpose.

Here is the biblical flow of prosperity:

1. Provide for Your Family: 1 Timothy 5:8 calls provision a faith responsibility.

2. Support Kingdom Work: Tithing, missions, church building, discipleship.

3. Bless the Poor: Psalm 41:1 promises reward to those who care for the poor.

4. Influence Culture and Systems: Joseph, Esther, Daniel, each used position, and resources to shape nations.

Wealth follows responsibility. God funds what He authors.

> Ask yourself: **What would I build or fund if money were no limit?**

Write it down.

Purpose breaks greed. It also pulls provision.

God has no problem pouring millions through you if He knows it will flow into purpose.

Would you provide to expand Kingdom objectives? Your vision determines your provision. God fills what you're willing to pour. The greater your "why," the stronger your "how."

This mindset kills greed at the root. You stop thinking, *"How much can I get?"* and start asking, *"How much can I give?"* And that shift breaks scarcity. Because the more you release, the more you make room for increase. Heaven doesn't flow through clenched fists; it flows through open hands.

Think about what would happen if every believer stopped seeing wealth as optional and started seeing it as a divine obligation. What if every Christian business owner tithed on their gross, not just their net? What if every artist, investor, and innovator used their success as seed for justice and revival? Entire nations would shift.

God has no problem making you a millionaire if He knows millions will move through you. He has no issue filling your account when He sees what you're willing to build, fund, and free. The issue is never access, it's assignment. When He finds people who see money as mission fuel, He pours without hesitation.

The phrase "Purpose-driven prosperity is unstoppable. God funds what He authors." encapsulates a profound truth about aligning one's financial endeavors with divine purpose. While the exact wording of this quote does not appear in widely recognized sources, it resonates with sentiments expressed by Christian leader Edwin Louis Cole, who stated:

> *"God will finish what He authors, but He is not obligated to finish what He has not authored."*—Edwin Louis Cole

This emphasizes that when God initiates a purpose or mission, He provides the necessary resources to see it through. Conversely, endeavors outside of His will may lack divine provision.

If you want to attract divine provision, align your prosperity with Kingdom objectives. Begin to declare over your life: *"I will be a conduit of blessing. I will fund what matters. I will prosper for a purpose bigger than me."* That is when abundance becomes sacred. That is when money becomes holy. That is when wealth fulfills its true assignment.

Your role in the Kingdom is too important to stay small. The vision God placed in you is too urgent to stay broke. The world needs your solution, your support, your strategy. So, rise, not just to be rich, but to be trusted. And when God finds you trustworthy, there is no limit to what He will release through your hands.

Examples of Wealthy Godly People in Scripture

The Bible is filled with wealthy people whom God trusted:

- **Abraham** – "very rich" in silver, gold, livestock

- **Isaac**– became "very wealthy" even during the famine

- **Jacob** – grew "exceedingly prosperous."

- **Joseph** – managed the wealth of a nation

- **David** – funded the Temple from personal treasure

- **Solomon** – global influence, unmatched wisdom

- **Job** – the greatest man of the East, he was doubly restored after a great misfortune

- **Lydia** – successful businesswoman; hosted the church

- **Women in Luke 8** – financed Jesus' ministry

- **Joseph of Arimathea** – a wealthy disciple who buried Jesus

- **Early church** – sold land and property to meet needs

The pattern is clear:

Wealth + righteousness = impact.

God still entrusts wealth to those who align with His purpose.

God has always entrusted wealth to those who aligned with His mission.

He is still doing it today. And He is looking for stewards with clean hands, clear purpose, and open hearts. Wealth in the right hands advances justice, establishes truth, and funds transformation. You don't need to fear it. You need to be prepared for it.

The same God who empowered Abraham, Joseph, Lydia, and the early church is still writing financial testimonies. The next one could be yours.

You are not chasing money.

You are stewarding a mission.

Now that you see wealth from God's view, the next question is simple:

How do you access it?

The first key: create value.

6

Value Creation: The Engine of Wealth

"You don't get paid by the hour. You get paid for the value you bring to the hour." – Jim Rohn

A woman began baking cookies in her kitchen during a tough season. She had no staff, no storefront, and no big plan. What she had was skill, consistency, and a product people loved. A local café asked to stock her cookies. Orders multiplied. Then contracts. Then distribution.

People were not paying for flour and sugar, they were paying for delight, taste, and consistency. She didn't just sell cookies. She solved a craving, created joy, and delivered quality. **That is value.**

Wealth does not chase potential.

It chases value.

When you solve problems, you unlock provision. The world rewards service, not effort. This message helps you tap into your God-given gifts and learn how value, solutions, and service open doors, just like Joseph, Daniel, and Jacob.

God gave you more than salvation. He gave you tools, talents, and wisdom. When you use them well, you create value that draws opportunities.

The Law of Service and Solutions

A problem is always looking for a solver. Every lasting business begins with service. The economy doesn't reward passion, it rewards solutions. When your passion solves something, your potential becomes profitable.

Wealth is not created by luck or prayer alone.

> **Wealth is the reward for service.**

Jesus taught it: *"Give, and it will be given to you..."* (Luke 6:38). This principle applies to generosity and value creation. When you increase your contribution, you increase your return.

If you want to raise your income, raise your impact.

Stop asking, "How can I make more money?"

Start asking, "Who can I serve today, and how well?"

Jesus modeled this.

He healed the sick, fed the hungry, taught with authority, and restored the broken. His value created trust, loyalty, and influence.

Elisha did the same. A widow needed help. All she had was a little oil. God used that oil to build a business and break her debt (2 Kings 4:1–7). Her value wasn't in what she lacked, but in what she offered.

Modern businesses do the same:

- Amazon solved slow delivery.

- Uber solved inconvenient transportation.

- Canva solved complicated design.

They did not chase trends, they solved problems. They identified consistent pain points and created scalable solutions.

This principle works in ministry, business, education, healthcare, and home. If your ministry solves nothing, it grows nothing. If your product or service helps no one, income will reflect it. Fruitfulness follows function.

Whose life improves because you exist?

That is where value begins.

Mini Activation

Write three common problems you see in your church, job, or community. Ask:

- Do I have experience or passion here?

- Could I offer a simpler or better solution?

- What small step can I test today?

Money is not magic. Money is a response.

When you become a solver, money finds you.

You were not born to chase money.

You were born to create value.

Your Gifts Make Room for You – Proverbs 18:16

A gift doesn't beg for recognition, it creates it. When your gift serves others with excellence, doors open. Proverbs 18:16 says a gift "makes room" and brings you before great people.

Your gift is not random.

It is Heaven's answer to Earth's problems.

Everyone carries a gift, teaching, organizing, creating, building, writing, speaking, healing, fixing, leading, nurturing. These are not hobbies. They are assignments.

In Matthew 25, the servant who buried his gift lost it. Fear, shame, and comparison will bury yours too. The enemy doesn't need to destroy your gift; he only needs you to devalue it.

Everyday people build businesses with what you call "ordinary."

- Your simple recipe

- Your daily devotional notes

- Your natural speaking ability

- Your eye for detail

- Your ability to organize

- Your love for helping people

The difference is not gifting, it is movement.

Your gift becomes valuable when you activate it, develop it, and use it with consistency.

Rockefeller once wrote, **"Action solves everything."**

Movement multiplies value.

Ask:

- What do people thank me for often?

- What feels natural to me?

- What gives me energy instead of draining it?

Your answers point to your assignment.

Joseph didn't apply to Pharaoh's palace. He used his gift in prison.

Daniel didn't beg for influence. His excellence brought kings to him.

You don't need to chase rooms.

Your gift will build the room.

You're not unqualified. You're undeployed.

Now is the time to uncover what God planted in you.

Don't wait until you feel worthy. Worth is never the issue, diligence in obedience is. The Kingdom isn't looking for polished performers. It's looking for committed stewards.

You were created to solve a problem.

Your gift is the strategy.

Your obedience is the accelerator.

Your impact is the reward.

Value in the Lives of Joseph, Daniel, and Jacob

In Scripture, value, not titles, brought wealth and influence.

1. Joseph

Joseph solved Pharaoh's dream *and* offered a national plan. His wisdom saved nations. He didn't demand promotion. Value found him. He interpreted dreams, but more importantly, he interpreted systems. He took a mystery and turned it into a national strategy. Pharaoh immediately promoted him to second-in-command. Joseph wasn't chasing power. He was solving problems. His value preserved entire nations.

2. Daniel

Daniel had an "excellent spirit." He solved problems no one else could solve. Kings kept him close because wisdom is rare. His brilliance wasn't confined to a tabernacle or his prayer closet. It shaped the decisions of empires. He didn't beg to be heard; his gift demanded it. Kings retained him because he brought clarity where others brought confusion. He added value, and it made him indispensable.

3. Jacob

Jacob multiplied livestock through strategy and divine insight. He was not wealthy because of inheritance. He had the blessing of his father, of course, but he became wealthy through strategy. He didn't steal from Laban; he outproduced him.

The pattern is clear:

- They didn't chase wealth.

- They offered solutions.

- Their value opened doors.

- Honor and provision followed.

They didn't enter palaces because they were favored.

They entered because they were valuable.

Proverbs 22:29 confirms this:

"Do you see a man skilled in his work? He will stand before kings."

That is not motivational fluff. It is a covenant truth.

If Joseph had been bitter, he would have missed the moment.

If Daniel had compromised, his voice would have lost weight.

If Jacob had been passive, he would have remained broke.

Value creates invitation.

Value attracts reward.

Value raises influence.

Developing Skills That Solve Problems

Talent is a gift.

Skill is a choice.

When you sharpen your skills, you multiply your value. Heaven responds to stewardship, not potential.

Every problem in the world needs someone with skill.

Skill is developed in four major areas:

1. Communication

Clear writing, speaking, listening, and persuading add immediate value.

2. Problem-Solving

People pay for clarity, direction, and solutions.

3. Technical Skills

Financial literacy, tech fluency, design, strategy, operations, these increase income and influence.

4. Relational Intelligence

Emotional health, teamwork, conflict resolution, and leadership are rare and rewarded.

Ask:

What one skill, if improved, would double my value?

Choose one. Develop it for 30 days.

Read. Practice. Ask for feedback.

Small steps create big shifts.

This is stewardship.

This is worship.

This is preparation for promotion.

Bezalel in Exodus was filled with the Spirit for craftsmanship.

God empowers skill, not laziness.

Solutions are waiting.

Promotion is waiting.

Your next level is waiting on your development.

Wealth doesn't chase noise.

It chases value.

And value grows when you sharpen your gift and serve with excellence.

Now that you know how to create value, the next step is learning how to **manage the wealth that follows.**

> *Financial Literacy and Stewardship* will show you how.

7

FINANCIAL LITERACY AS A KINGDOM DISCIPLINE

"It's not your salary that makes you rich, it's your spending habits."
—*Charles A. Jaffe*

Winning the lottery does not guarantee freedom. Most lottery winners file for bankruptcy within a few years (Kaplan, 2010). Not because they lack opportunity, but because they lack understanding. **Wealth in the hands of someone untrained becomes a burden, not a blessing.**

You don't rise by miracle alone.

You rise through management.

Many believers know how to tithe and give. Few know how to budget, save, invest, or multiply. Wealth grows only when it is managed well.

This chapter gives you tools that turn spiritual momentum into financial momentum. You will see why wealth is not just income. You will learn how to manage money like someone building a legacy, not surviving a paycheck.

You will discover why God cares how you handle what He gives. You will learn the difference between ownership and stewardship, why budgeting is spiritual warfare, and how to grow financial intelligence in your home.

God doesn't want you blessed only.

He wants you equipped.

Stewardship vs. Ownership

Most people think their money belongs to them. *My paycheck. My savings. My investments.* That mindset leads to shallow decisions and small impact.

Scripture corrects this idea:

"The earth is the Lord's, and everything in it." —Psalm 24:1

That includes every dollar you have.

You are not the owner; you are the manager.

When you believe you own it, you spend for comfort.

When you believe God owns it, you spend with purpose.

This shift changes everything.

Stewardship turns spending into worship.

It makes giving intentional.

It makes budgeting spiritual.

Jesus said:

"Whoever can be trusted with very little can also be trusted with much..." —Luke 16:10

Stewardship attracts increase. Ownership breeds pressure.

Joseph modeled this in Egypt.

Pharaoh owned the grain.

Joseph managed it with wisdom.

His stewardship saved a nation.

When you see your bank account as God's resource, you spend differently. You tithe with joy. You pause before buying. You ask, *"Is this how God wants His money used?"*

That is maturity.

Stewards live with peace.

Owners live with pressure.

Stewards expect increase.

Owners fear loss.

Every paycheck is a test.

Every dollar is an assignment.

You are not just making money.

You are multiplying purpose.

Budgeting, Saving, and Managing Money God's Way

The moment income hits your account, you face a choice: intention or drift. Money goes where you direct it, or where you let it slip away.

"The plans of the diligent lead to profit…" —**Proverbs 21:5**

A budget is not punishment.

It is a blueprint for purpose.

It answers two questions:

1. What has God placed in my hands?

2. What does He want done with it?

Saving is spiritual too. Proverbs 6 praises the ant for storing during harvest. Saving creates margin. It prepares you for opportunity and protects you in crisis. Budgeting is not punishment. It's a form of vision that says that "I refuse to let today rob tomorrow."

A simple framework: **The 10–10–10-70 Model**

This builds discipline and peace.

Budgeting tools like **YNAB** or **Mint** can help.

Or use a simple envelope system, when an envelope is empty, you stop spending.

Set clear financial goals:

- **Short-term**: Pay off one bill. Save for a small purchase.

- **Mid-term**: Build an emergency fund.

- **Long-term**: Home ownership. Retirement. Business funding.

"When you don't tell your money where to go, it tells you where it went."

Budgeting gives every dollar a mission.

Example income: **$2,000**

- $200 tithe

- $200 save

- $200 invest

- $1,400 live on

Break the $1,400 into categories, rent, utilities, food, transportation, giving, fun, etc.

This is not about perfection.

It is about order.

Prayer opens the heavens.

Planning protects the harvest.

God will not override poor habits.

Financial peace comes from structure, not emotion.

If you want increase, start with order.

Stewardship prepares you for more.

Understanding Assets vs. Liabilities

Wealth doesn't begin with how much you earn.

It begins with how much you keep, and how your money works for you.

Robert Kiyosaki explains:

- **Assets put money in your pocket.**

- **Liabilities take money out.**

Examples of **assets**:

- Rental property

- Dividend stocks

- A business

- Royalties or digital products

Examples of **liabilities**:

- Car loans

- Consumer debt

- Your home (if it produces no income)

- High-cost lifestyle spending

Many people work for money, then buy liabilities that drain them. A new car looks like success but costs hundreds each month. Meanwhile, a small investment planted early could grow for decades.

Do a simple audit:

Column 1: What builds wealth?

Column 2: What drains money?

You'll see the truth quickly.

This is not guilt, it's clarity.

Wisdom builds wealth.

Emotion destroys it.

Start small. Move $20, $50, or $100 from liabilities into assets each month. Even a book or course is an asset when it increases your earning ability.

Wealth is not magic.

It is math guided by wisdom.

Financial wisdom is about choosing future gain over present appearance.

Overcoming Financial Illiteracy in the Church

Many believers tithe and give faithfully yet stay financially stuck. Not because they lack generosity, but because they lack training.

> *"My people perish for lack of knowledge."* —**Hosea 4:6**

Churches often teach giving but not management. People sow seeds but don't know how to store or multiply the harvest.

Generosity is not a replacement for stewardship.

Both are required.

Luke 16:11 challenges us:

"If you're not trustworthy with worldly wealth, who will trust you with true riches?"

Churches must teach:

- Budgeting

- Debt reduction

- Saving

- Investing

- Entrepreneurship

- Estate planning

Godly people cannot carry Kingdom influence while trapped in financial chaos.

Jesus taught more about money than heaven or hell because money shapes decisions, emotions, and faith.

Financial literacy in the church produces:

- Debt freedom

- Strong families

- Bold givers

- Marketplace leaders

- Multi-generational legacy

This is Kingdom culture, not secular theory.

When faith meets wisdom, prosperity becomes sustainable.

You now know how to manage what God gives.

In the next chapter, you'll learn how to expand your vision.

God is not limited. His Kingdom operates in overflow.

8

THE ECONOMICS OF ABUNDANCE

"Blessed be the Lord, who daily loads us with benefits, the God of our salvation!" (Psalms 68:19, NKJV)

Why do God's children, who have access to the Source of all things, live as if there isn't enough? Why do so many who believe in Heaven's power still operate from fear, limitation, and small thinking? The issue rarely begins in the wallet. It starts in the mind.

Abundance is not reserved for a select few. It is a divine reality secured for every believer through covenant. Lack is not your portion. Scarcity is not a badge of humility. Overflow is your inheritance, and abundance is your birthright in Christ.

The greatest obstacle to abundance is not external, it is internal. Abundance does not start with money. It starts with mindset. If you see God as limited, you will always settle for scraps. If you believe there is never enough, you will shrink, hoard, and stay small, no matter how much God pours into your life.

This chapter breaks that ceiling. We will dismantle the deception of scarcity, reveal the nature of God's Kingdom, shift from fear to faith, and show how to activate overflow through the power of your words.

Abundance isn't distant. It's already within reach. Let's align your thinking with what Heaven has already released.

Scarcity is a Lie

Scarcity is a lie dressed as logic. It disguises itself as responsibility, humility, or practicality, but underneath it is fear. It whispers, "There's not enough", not enough money, opportunities, clients, land, favor, resources, or open doors. And when you believe that voice, limitation follows, even when Heaven has declared overflow.

God never introduced scarcity. In the beginning, He created a garden overflowing with provision. Trees were abundant. Rivers supplied everything Adam needed. Scarcity came after sin, not before. It is a post-fall condition, not a Kingdom mindset.

God reveals Himself as El Shaddai — "The All-Sufficient One." He does not just meet needs; He exceeds them. That is why Psalm 34:10 says, "Those who seek the Lord lack no good thing." The promise is not survival but sufficiency.

Jesus reinforced this in John 10:10. He came so we could have life "more abundantly", a phrase meaning "beyond measure." Lack was never the plan.

Scarcity mindsets are often inherited. Some grew up in homes where survival shaped beliefs. Others absorbed teachings that glorified poverty. Many were taught that desiring more meant being less spiritual. Over time, these beliefs limit what we expect, believe, and act on.

Scarcity produces fear-based decisions. It tells you to hoard instead of sow, shrink instead of build, and play safe instead of obey boldly. It breeds jealousy because it convinces you someone else's gain reduces your chances. It makes people settle, asking for a corner when God offered the land.

But Heaven never operates in lack. God isn't budgeting blessings. He isn't limited by inflation or markets. His provision flows from His character.

> Scarcity is not humility. It is bondage. True humility agrees with what God says, and God calls Himself abundant.

You do not honor God by living beneath your inheritance. You honor Him by receiving what He has made available, stewarding it with wisdom, and using it to bless others. Scarcity ends when you agree with what Heaven believes about you.

God's Kingdom Is Unlimited

God doesn't think in limits; He speaks in overflow. Everything He creates carries the imprint of abundance. Genesis 1 shows creation bursting with variety. He didn't make one tree, He made thousands. He didn't fill the oceans with a few fish, He filled them with living diversity. Supply, not lack, was built into the blueprint.

Revelation 21:21 describes streets of gold in Heaven. That is not excess, it is design. What earth calls precious, Heaven calls pavement.

In Luke 5:6, Jesus filled Peter's boat with so many fish it began to sink. Peter didn't ask for that much; he simply obeyed. The result was overflow. Jesus did the same with water turned to wine and the feeding of the five thousand. He didn't give "just enough", He demonstrated Kingdom supply.

Ephesians 3:20 defines the culture of God's Kingdom: "exceedingly, abundantly above all that we ask or think."

God's abundance isn't greed. It's His nature. When you align your faith with His scale, small prayers start sounding unfamiliar.

Stop praying for survival. Start believing for vision, legacy, and impact. Scarcity ends where revelation begins.

Shifting from Fear to Faith

Fear often sounds like wisdom. It uses logic, caution, and reason, but its root message is the same: "There's not enough."

Fear keeps people in survival mode. It highlights limitations and risk. It shuts down generosity and paralyzes opportunity. Fear is not responsible, it is expensive.

Faith sees the same numbers but sees promise instead of pressure. Hebrews 11:6 says faith pleases God. Kingdom finance requires it. God partners with belief, not fear.

Jesus taught this in Matthew 6:25–34. Birds are fed. Lilies are clothed. Your Father knows your needs. Instead of chasing provision, seek His Kingdom, and "all these things" follow.

Fear says, "I can't afford that."

Faith says, "God will supply my needs."

Fear says, "What if I fail?"

Faith says, "What if this is my breakthrough?"

Fear hoards. Faith releases.

Fear clings. Faith sows.

Fear hesitates. Faith moves.

Take action now:

Write down three areas where fear directs your financial decisions. Then write a bold faith confession to replace each one. Speak them aloud until your mind aligns with Heaven's economy.

> Your transformation begins where fear ends.

Speaking Abundance Over Your Life

Abundance begins in your vocabulary.

Proverbs 18:21 says life and death are in the power of the tongue. Your words create the framework for what you expect, tolerate, and manifest. Your mouth is a construction tool.

You cannot think poverty, speak lack, and walk in overflow. Heaven responds to agreement. When your words align with God's promises, you activate what He has released.

God spoke creation into being. Jesus spoke to storms, fig trees, and situations. Ezekiel was commanded to prophesy, not analyze.

You were made in the image of a speaking God. Your voice carries creative authority, not because of positivity, but because of Kingdom alignment.

If your words shape your world, then speaking fear will build a fearful world. Speaking abundance builds an environment where overflow can land.

Here are seven declarations for the next 30 days:

- "I walk in the overflow of God."

- "There is more than enough for my assignment."

- "I attract Kingdom opportunities and provision."

- "My cup overflows with divine favor."

- "I am not limited by economy; I am resourced by Heaven."

- "I don't compete, I create."

- "My faith multiplies what I steward."

Don't just read them, release them. Speak boldly. Write them down. Post them. Record them. These are not motivational phrases; they are spiritual weapons.

Speak until your soul believes.

Speak until fear weakens.

Speak until lack loses its voice.

Your words are not just prayers; they are creative tools in the Kingdom economy.

Scarcity has no authority in the Kingdom. It contradicts your Father's nature. Faith opens what fear shuts. Your words act as gates. What you speak shapes what you live.

You were not made for barely enough. You were created to multiply in God's abundance.

And abundance thrives in an atmosphere of thankfulness. If you want the flow to continue, the next key is gratitude.

9

THE GRATITUDE ADVANTAGE

"Gratitude is not only the greatest of virtues, but the parent of all the others." – Cicero

"In everything give thanks; for this is the will of God in Christ Jesus for you." (1 Thessalonians 5:18, NKJV)

A gift unacknowledged often becomes a gift withheld. If someone kept receiving from you but never expressed thanks, no smile, no honor, no recognition, your motivation to give again would fade. Gratitude unlocks more. Not because God needs affirmation, but because thankfulness reveals maturity and readiness for increase.

Gratitude is more than a good attitude. It's a spiritual technology. It multiplies resources, anchors your focus, and sharpens your awareness of God's hand at work in your finances. When you give thanks, you're not just saying "thank you." You're building an environment for continued overflow.

This chapter will walk you through the practical and supernatural power of thanksgiving. You'll see how gratitude partners with multiplication, how it separates stewardship from entitlement, and how you can build a habit of journaling and declaring God's provision with intention. You'll also confront the subtle ways entitlement can block your breakthrough, and how to shift into a posture that invites favor and faith to flow freely.

If you want to increase what you carry, you must honor what you've already been given. Gratitude is the gateway to more. Let's unlock it.

Gratitude Attracts Increase

Gratitude is more than good manners. It's a multiplier. Heaven responds to thanksgiving not as courtesy, but as spiritual intelligence. When you give thanks, you activate the divine pattern that turns little into more.

Jesus never treated thanksgiving as optional. Before feeding the multitudes with seven loaves and a few fish, He paused to give thanks. "And He took the seven loaves and the fish, and giving thanks, He broke them..." (Matthew 15:36). Only after gratitude came multiplication. The supernatural didn't follow the request; it followed the recognition.

In John 11:41, before Lazarus walked out of the tomb, Jesus thanked the Father: "Father, I thank You that You have heard Me." He didn't wait for the miracle to manifest. He thanked God in advance, and resurrection followed.

The same rhythm appears in Psalm 67:5–6: praise first, increase second. Increase is not random. It follows gratitude. The earth responds to thanksgiving. The invisible realm begins to open when your heart does.

What you're thankful for, you permit to multiply. What you ignore or complain about, you push away. Gratitude is not passive appreciation. It is an aggressive faith response that honors God's hand even before you see His harvest.

Science confirms what the Word has always declared. Gratitude increases dopamine and serotonin, the brain's "reward" chemicals. It strengthens immune response, enhances creativity, and boosts resilience (Emmons & Stern, 2013).

Thanksgiving shifts your perspective and your possibility. It helps you spot opportunities others miss because you're tuned to abundance, not lack.

Gratitude also reframes your experience. What once felt insufficient suddenly looks like seed. You stop asking, "Why isn't this enough?" and start declaring, "Thank You for trusting me with the beginning of something great."

One of the most powerful ways to break stagnation is to give thanks for where you are, what you have, and what God is forming in you right now. Thank Him for the job before the promotion. Thank Him for the client before the contract. Thank Him for the gift before the audience.

What if your increase is waiting on your appreciation? What if heaven is holding a harvest until gratitude opens the gate? The sooner you start thanking, the sooner you start multiplying.

Thankfulness Unlocks More

Ten men cried out to Jesus for mercy. As they went, they were healed. But only one returned to say thank you.

"Were not ten cleansed?" Jesus asked. "Where are the other nine?" (Luke 17:17–18). Then He told the grateful one: "Rise and go; your faith has made you whole." (Luke 17:19).

The nine were healed. The one was made whole.

Healing touched the surface. Wholeness touched the story. Wholeness restores what was lost and marks you with favor that touches other areas. Thankfulness turned one miracle into a doorway for more.

Gratitude is not just polite. It signals readiness for the next level. God doesn't just respond to faith; He responds to thanksgiving. He multiplies in the hands of those who return.

Ingratitude is subtle mismanagement. It silently says, "This wasn't enough." And what is not honored will not be multiplied.

When you fail to recognize God's hand in the small, you disqualify yourself from more. Increase is not tested in overflow but in moments of small beginnings, a $100 check, a kind word, a single client. Heaven watches how you respond.

Gratitude for the little is not weakness. It is wisdom. It shows God you won't waste what He gives you. That you see His fingerprints even when the picture is unfinished. That you measure His goodness by His faithfulness, not by the size of the gift.

Gratitude doesn't mean settling. It means you're mature enough for more.

If you want enlargement, enlarge your thanks. Blessings grow where there is honor. The ones who return are the ones who rise.

Journaling and Testifying God's Provision

Your breakthrough is not only in what you pray, but in what you remember. One of the strongest weapons against fear and scarcity is your testimony. "They overcame... by the word of their testimony." (Revelation 12:11).

Testimonies are not meant to be lost. They are meant to be written and spoken. Habakkuk 2:2 says, "Write the vision." The same applies to your testimonies. What you don't write down, you forget. What you forget, you stop praising. What you stop praising, you stop expecting.

Start a Gratitude Journal or a Wealth Testimony Tracker. Write three things each day that God has provided: answered prayers, unexpected income, ideas, opportunities, favor, discounts, or peace during pressure.

This trains your eyes to see supply. You realize abundance is not rare, it's constant.

Don't keep testimonies to yourself. Share them. Speak them in small groups or with partners. Your words stir faith in others and multiply the atmosphere for miracles.

Make it a weekly habit: write one "money testimony" every week for 90 days. Watch how expectation rises. Watch how clarity grows. You'll realize you weren't waiting on provision; provision was waiting on your attention.

> Testimony is a weapon. Write it. Say it. Share it. The more you testify of God's goodness, the more you live in the overflow of it.

Gratitude vs Entitlement in Wealth

Entitlement chokes blessing. It convinces you that what you have is owed to you, and what others have should be yours. Gratitude and entitlement cannot coexist. One multiplies. The other blocks.

Entitlement says, "God owes me."

Gratitude says, "God has already blessed me beyond what I deserve."

Jesus illustrated this in Luke 15. The elder brother had access to everything, yet entitlement blinded him from seeing it. He resented, compared, and felt overlooked.

That's what entitlement does. It focuses on what you lack. It breeds comparison, jealousy, and bitterness. It whispers that God favors others more. It convinces you to withhold gratitude until the blessing is big enough or impressive enough.

Gratitude shifts your lens. It rejoices in others' harvest. It thanks God for the seed and the soil. It celebrates progress, not just results. It knows every open door starts with a thank-you for a cracked window.

If bitterness rises when others are blessed, or if you feel stuck or overlooked, it may be time to reject entitlement and choose gratitude.

Break it by:

• Celebrating others sincerely

• Thanking God for small things

• Praising before the breakthrough

• Blessing even when it feels unfair

Declare this:

"I am not entitled. I am entrusted. I honor what I've been given and thank God in all things. My gratitude is a magnet for miracles. I rejoice when others are blessed because my time is coming too."

Gratitude keeps the Kingdom economy alive in your life. Entitlement shuts it down.

Gratitude is more than a feeling; it is a force. It opens doors effort cannot open. It multiplies what you honor and steadies your heart in seasons of waiting. Thankfulness doesn't wait for overflow, it attracts it. Journaling builds a record of God's faithfulness. Entitlement erodes expectation. Every increase begins with appreciation.

When you posture your heart in gratitude, God can trust you with more because you know who the Source is.

You now have the laws. Next, we'll build your personal blueprint. Let's move from understanding to implementation and construct a wealth system that lasts.

10

STRATEGIC WEALTH ARCHITECTURE

"Through wisdom a house is built, and by understanding it is established; by knowledge the rooms are filled with rare and beautiful treasure." – Proverbs 24:3–4

If God placed a million dollars in your hand today, do you have a plan for it? If not, the issue may not be provision, but preparation. Wealth flows toward structure. It follows vision. Many believers cry out for increase without preparing for what they've already asked God to release.

Heaven responds to faith, but it also honors design. God gave Moses exact dimensions for the Tabernacle. Noah received specific instructions for the ark. Joseph built a seven-year storage plan that saved nations. These were not random acts of obedience. They were acts of strategy. Divine outcomes require intentional structure.

Wealth is not sustained by emotion or momentum. It requires wisdom, clarity, and simple systems. Financial breakthrough happens where faith meets stewardship. Without planning, increase has nowhere to settle.

This chapter will walk you through the practical systems needed to build and sustain Kingdom wealth. You'll learn how to craft a personal financial blueprint, align your giving with purpose, lay the foundation for basic investments, and scale your finances with growth-oriented planning.

The goal is not complexity. It is clarity. As you implement these tools, you'll stop praying for harvests your field is not prepared to hold. Strategy is not a substitute for grace. It is how grace moves through action. Heaven is ready to release. This chapter equips you to receive.

Creating a Kingdom Financial Plan

Most people spend more time planning a vacation than planning their financial future. Yet the Word is clear: *"Write the vision and make it plain."* (Habakkuk 2:2). That includes money. Financial vision is spiritual stewardship. You cannot multiply what you have not planned for.

Money moves toward clarity. Confusion repels provision. Heaven does not respond to random wishes. It responds to aligned faith, structured purpose, and responsible action.

A Kingdom financial plan is not a spreadsheet of anxiety. It is a written act of covenant alignment. It says, *"I take responsibility for what I have, and I'm preparing for what God wants to release."*

Your plan is not about survival. It is a tool to build wealth, fund vision, honor God, bless family, and create generational impact. Kingdom wealth flows through systems. Strategy brings sustainability.

A full financial plan includes key components:

Income: List current income and expected income. Include both active and passive streams. Clarity here creates direction.

Giving: Outline your tithe pattern, generosity goals, and assignments. Do not leave giving to chance. Budget your generosity with intention.

Debt Strategy: List every debt, interest rate, and payoff plan. Decide what you will attack first. Set timelines, not vague wishes.

Saving Goals: Include emergency funds, short-term goals, and long-term purpose savings (business launches, vision projects, real estate). Saving is not hoarding. It is how wisdom prepares.

Investment Buckets: Decide where you want your money to grow, real estate, business, stocks, or Kingdom-focused funds. Begin learning and assigning portions toward growth.

Legacy Planning: Create or review your will. Explore trusts or financial vehicles that transfer wealth with wisdom. Legacy is not money left behind. It is wisdom passed forward.

Take 30 minutes and create a one-page plan. Answer four simple questions:

1. What do I have?

2. What do I owe?

3. What do I need to build?

4. Where is God leading me?

Writing creates structure. Structure invites increase. Without a plan, increase frustrates. With a plan, increase empowers.

You cannot steward what you have not defined. Take the time. Get the clarity. Build the structure. God is not waiting for you to beg; He is waiting for you to build.

The Role of Tithing and Giving

Giving is not random. It is spiritual architecture. Many treat giving as emotional or religious, but Kingdom giving is structured, intentional, and covenantal. It is worship and wisdom. It aligns your financial life with Heaven's economy.

Malachi 3:10 makes this clear: "Bring the full tithe into the storehouse... and see if I will not open for you the windows of heaven." Tithing is not legalism. It is alignment. It connects your heart to Heaven's system and your income to supernatural supply.

Tithing is the first 10% of all increase. It is not charity. It is covenant recognition. You declare, *"God, You are my Source."* Tithing does not buy favor. It honors partnership. It brings the remaining 90% under blessing.

Offerings come next, freewill, sacrificial gifts that express love, gratitude, or obedience. These may support missions, leaders, building projects, or Spirit-led opportunities. Luke 6:38 shows that offering activates reciprocal Kingdom flow.

First fruits are the first portion of a new stream, your first paycheck, bonus, or new revenue. You say, "God, You get the first before I touch the rest."

Alms are gifts to the poor and vulnerable. These are compassion gifts, not investment gifts. Jesus said they should be given in secret. Alms attract divine favor because they reflect God's heart.

Each giving type has a purpose. When you blur them, you mismanage the power. You do not sow where you should give alms. You do not tithe as if it were charity. Each has a design.

Giving must be planned. Not squeezed into leftovers. Set percentages. Create monthly goals. Align generosity with assignment.

Spontaneous giving has its place. But sustained, powerful generosity requires structure. Intentional giving is lasting giving.

Giving was never meant to be random. It breaks greed, assigns purpose to money, and positions you for divine flow. When you give with understanding, you do not lose. You multiply.

Investment 101 (Real Estate, Stocks, Business)

God expects multiplication. In Matthew 25:27, the master rebuked the servant for not growing what he was given. Unused money loses value. Money in motion grows.

Investing is stewardship. It is not greed. It is wisdom at work. Jesus honored increase, not hoarding.

Believers should understand three main vehicles:

1. Real Estate

Real estate is one of the oldest forms of wealth. It builds wealth through appreciation, cash flow, and tax advantages.

Abraham insisted on buying land for Sarah's burial. Land was legacy. It still is.

Real estate can be passive (REITs) or active (rentals, flipping, commercial leases). It is slow but powerful. It offers leverage and stability.

Begin with education. Learn mortgages, taxes, tenant law, and local markets. Real estate is responsibility.

2. Stocks & Markets

Stock ownership means owning part of a company. Returns come through appreciation and dividends. The market is volatile in the short term but strong over long periods.

Start small. Learn before you leap. Use fractional shares if needed.

Believers can also use faith-based investment screeners to avoid supporting ungodly agendas.

3. Entrepreneurship / Business

Most biblical wealth came through business activity, Abraham, Lydia, Proverbs 31, Paul, even Jesus as a carpenter.

Business is solving problems with products or services. It is value creation.

Start with what you know. What do people ask you for? What comes naturally? What problems can you solve?

Start small and smart. Build with integrity. Business becomes ministry when done with excellence.

Activation Exercise

Pick one action this month:

- Research real estate, stocks, or business.

- Identify a mentor, book, or course.

- Take one step: open a brokerage account, attend a workshop, draft a business concept.

You do not need to master all three. Pick one door and move. God multiplies what you move.

Investing is not a race. It is a partnership between wisdom, diligence, and faith. With God as strategist and the Spirit as guide, your investments become eternal.

Budgeting and Planning for Growth

Budgeting is how faith takes structure. Proverbs 21:5 says, "The plans of the diligent lead to abundance."

A budget is stewardship. It is preparation for increase. Many want miracles but ignore clarity. But miracles do not replace strategy.

A Kingdom budget is a vision map. It tells your money where to go. It brings peace and direction.

Start with monthly cash flow:

- What comes in?

- What goes out?

- Are you living above or below your margin?

Most people do not need more money first. They need more management.

> Think beyond survival. Build a growth budget. What will it take to hire help, expand business, or grow ministry? Growth must be priced before it is prayed for.

When income rises, grow your margin, not just your lifestyle. Upgrade giving, saving, and investing before you upgrade possessions.

Plan for expenses at future income levels. Reinvest in your business. Do not drain momentum too early.

Set generosity goals. Increase giving as God increases you.

Entrepreneurs should plan for team building. Vision grows with people.

Audit your budget this week. Ask:

- Where is the leak?

- What is underfunded?

- What has no Kingdom purpose?

Circle what needs cutting. Highlight what needs support. Underline what needs vision.

If your budget doesn't include growth, you are managing survival. You were called to the Promised Land, not stuck in financial Egypt.

The Discipline of Hard Work

Faith and favor are real. But so is sweat. Work is worship with the right heart.

Proverbs says the diligent are supplied. Hunger without effort is fantasy.

Hard work does not replace grace. It partners with it. Paul said he worked harder than others, but it was grace working in him.

Wealth flows through consistent hands, not just gifted ones.

Gifting opens the door.

Grit keeps you in the room.

Talking about ideas does nothing. Working on them moves life forward.

The Bible honors workers. Ruth gleaned. David tended sheep. Joseph managed houses and prisons. Faithfulness in labor came before leadership.

This is not burnout. It is daily stewardship. Put your hands to what God assigned.

Ask yourself:

- Where have I been praying but not producing?

- What vision have I spoken but not built?

Miracles come to movers. Favor accelerates the faithful. God won't build the ark, but He will guide the wood and rain.

Wisdom builds wealth. Strategy sustains it. God blesses what is prepared.

A Kingdom plan is a prophetic blueprint. It reflects what you believe about God and your assignment. Giving and investing are not opposites. One releases. The other multiplies.

Plan for growth, not just bills. Give every dollar an assignment. Pray and plan. Both are needed.

You are not just called to wealth. You are called to build it wisely.

Now that your foundation is set, it's time to multiply your streams. Let's explore how multiple income flows protect and accelerate your Kingdom wealth.

11

DESIGNING AND MANAGING MULTIPLE INCOME STREAMS

"Never depend on a single income. Make investments to create a second source." – Warren Buffett

If one income stream disappeared today, would your household stay steady or collapse? Most people live closer to financial disruption than they realize. One shift in the economy, one health issue, or one job loss can expose how prepared, or unprepared, they really are.

Scripture shows a better way. Ecclesiastes 11:2 urges us to divide our portion among many. God's wisdom has always included diversification, not for greed, but for protection.

In today's world, multiple income streams are no longer optional. Whether you're a teacher, entrepreneur, creative, or ministry leader, you were not designed to stay in one financial lane. You were designed to multiply.

This chapter will help you move beyond paycheck dependence. You'll learn the difference between active and passive income, how to build a Kingdom business rooted in purpose, and how to monetize the gifts God placed in you. You don't need ten incomes today; you need a clear path forward.

Let's build your next stream with wisdom, faith, and strategy.

Why One Stream Is Too Risky

One income stream may feel secure, until it stops. No one plans for layoffs, sickness, or economic shifts, yet these moments often come without warning. When a single stream dries up, panic follows if nothing else is in place.

Ecclesiastes 11:2 tells us, *"Give a portion to seven, and also to eight, for you do not know what disaster may come upon the land."* God's people were never meant to depend on one channel. Diversification protects what He provides.

During COVID-19, millions lost work overnight. Yet people with a digital product, freelance skill, or passive income survived. Teachers sold resources online. Musicians taught virtual lessons. Leaders with books saw them become both income and ministry tools.

When income is tied to one employer or one business, you're only one disruption away from instability. Multiple streams act like financial insurance. If one is shaken, the others carry you.

The wealthy diversify because it protects their future. This is not greed, it is wisdom. And Jesus affirmed this in the Parable of the Talents. Those who multiplied were trusted with more.

You already have something God can bless, a skill, experience, or insight. Write down your current stream, then ask:

What other ways can I serve, teach, sell, or build that align with my calling?

Your financial future is shaped by how many ways you allow God to flow through your life. When you multiply streams, you multiply peace.

Passive Income and Active Income

Every believer should understand the difference between income that stops when you stop and income that keeps producing after the work is done.

Active income is earned when you work, jobs, consulting, coaching, or freelance projects. If you stop, the income stops.

Passive income is different. It begins with effort, writing a book, creating a course, investing in real estate, licensing your music or tools, and then continues producing without daily labor. It takes time, but it brings stability and freedom.

Deuteronomy 28:12 says, *"The Lord will bless all the work of your hands."* God blesses what you build once and release as seed. That seed continues to bear fruit long after the planting.

Scripture shows both models.

- The Proverbs 31 woman worked actively but also owned a vineyard, an asset.

- Paul preached and traveled but also made tents.

- Both streams supported their assignments.

The goal is not choosing one or the other. It's learning to build both. Most people start with active income, that's where skill and discipline are formed. But as you mature, you convert knowledge, experience, or capital into systems that produce.

This is not chasing shortcuts. Passive income is the reward of wisdom and structure.

Start with one question:

- **How can I multiply what I already know or have?**

- Could you create a guide? A course? A devotional? A downloadable resource?

- Write down one skill you've mastered and one way it could earn while you rest.

Active income pays your bills.

Passive income funds your vision.

Both honor God when built with purpose.

How to Launch a Kingdom Business

You were not created only to work inside someone else's vision. You were designed to create solutions, solve problems, and reflect God's excellence in the marketplace. Business began in Eden, through stewarding, naming, and cultivating.

A Kingdom business is not built on hype or greed. It is built on clarity and service.

Start with one question: What problem do you solve?

Great businesses solve clear problems, websites, baked goods, tutoring, coaching, designs, consulting. Someone is waiting for what you've mastered.

After clarity, test your idea. Who needs what you offer? Ask questions. Get feedback. Start small. Don't build systems without confirming the need.

Next, package your value into one simple offer, a product, service, membership, or workshop. Simplicity sells. Clarity brings clients.

Price your offer with confidence. People pay for solutions, not confusion. Ask God for wisdom in pricing. Never let fear discount what faith built.

Market your work with integrity. Tell real stories. Share real results. People respond to transformation, not hype. Let your clients testify. Let your work speak.

Then build basic systems, payments, delivery, onboarding, communication. You don't need everything at once, but you need something stable enough to grow.

A Kingdom business is not a side hustle. It is a multiplication tool God can breathe on. It can fund churches, free families, and change communities.

Action Step:

Write three problems you can solve. Pick one and outline a simple offer. What would it look like to serve five people this month? Start small. Build well. Let God multiply it.

Monetizing Your God-Given Skills

"A man's gift makes room for him and brings him before great men." – Proverbs 18:16

Some of your best income streams are already in your hands. They are found in what you do with ease, what others thank you for, and what you enjoy solving.

Value is created when your gift solves someone else's problem.

Many everyday people have built strong income streams by simply packaging what they already know.

- Teachers sell digital worksheets.

- Parents turn meal prep into coaching.

- Retired professionals mentor the next generation.

- These aren't celebrities, they're people who noticed their gift carried value.

Monetizing your skill is not twisting your calling for profit. It is releasing your solution to those who need it.

There are many models:

- Speaking, coaching, consulting

- Digital courses, templates, or guides

- Books, devotionals, or journals

- Paid communities or mentorship groups

- Creative services like music, editing, or design

- Your gift is a seed. When packaged with wisdom, it produces fruit.

Start with clarity:

What do others ask you for?

What comes naturally to you?

What have you overcome that others still struggle with?

Your gift matters to someone. And when your gift is stewarded well, it becomes both ministry and marketplace impact.

Wealth multiplies under wisdom. One income stream exposes you to risk. Multiple streams build stability, opportunity, and peace.

Active income gives momentum.

Passive income gives margin.

Both matter in Kingdom wealth.

A Kingdom business is not about popularity, it's about impact, service, and obedience. And your gift is not for storage, it's for stewardship.

When you release what God placed in your hands, you step into a life of multiplication.

12

Avoiding the Pitfalls That Sabotage Wealth

"It's not how much money you make, but how much you keep, how hard it works for you, and how many generations you keep it for."
—Robert Kiyosaki

Plenty of people reach six figures, yet very few keep it. The problem is not always income, the problem is protection. Wealth must not only be created. It must be guarded. Creation is half the work. Protection decides longevity.

The biggest threats to your wealth often look harmless. They show up as emotions, impulse choices, and habits that go unchecked. Most people don't lose wealth because of demons. They lose it through poor judgment and misplaced desires.

Scripture warns us in Proverbs 22:3:

"The prudent see danger and take refuge, but the simple keep going and pay the penalty."

Financial trouble is not always a mystery. There are patterns and traps. And God gives wisdom so you can see them and avoid them.

This chapter exposes four major destroyers of Kingdom wealth:

- Debt cycles

- Get-rich-quick temptation

- Emotional spending

- Comparison and greed

These are not simple errors; they become spiritual strongholds if left untouched. Every wealth builder must learn to guard the gates. This is where spiritual wisdom meets practical boundaries. If you want to keep what God gives you, you must guard it —not with fear, but with strategy.

Let's expose these traps one by one.

Debt Cycles and Financial Bondage

A raise will not break the bondage of debt. Only wisdom will. Many people pray for increase, yet ignore the silent drain of interest, late fees, and stress. It is not always a lack of income that destroys wealth. Often, it's unmanaged debt eating away at the inside.

Proverbs 22:7 says, **"The borrower is slave to the lender."**

Debt without boundaries becomes bondage. It shifts a Kingdom heir into the posture of a financial servant.

Not all debt is evil. But:

- Borrowing without a plan

- Spending without clarity

- And using credit to maintain a lifestyle... these create chains.

Credit cards used "for emergencies" turn into lifestyle crutches.

Student loans without a strategy become silent stress.

Personal loans taken to impress others become heavy burdens.

The cycle is predictable:

Debt → Stress → Delayed goals → Emotional spending → More debt.

What began as a tool becomes a trap.

Many believers sow, tithe, attend church and still feel stuck. The issue is often stewardship, not generosity. **Giving is not a replacement for budgeting.** Miracles do not excuse mismanagement. Wisdom guards the harvest.

Freedom begins with facing the numbers.

List every debt.

Know the total.

Then create a plan using:

- **Snowball method** (smallest to largest debts)

- **Avalanche method** (highest interest first)

Even small progress builds momentum.

Reduce excess. Cancel unused subscriptions. Cut emotional purchases. Remove anything that drains purpose and delays freedom.

Debt is not just math —it is mindset.

Speak over your finances:

"I am a steward, not a slave. I will not serve debt. I serve destiny."

Freedom begins in the will. Once your will aligns, your wallet follows.

1. Get-Rich-Quick Deceptions

Shortcuts look exciting. They promise speed without sacrifice. But shortcuts steal more than they give.

Proverbs 13:11 warns: **"Wealth gained hastily will dwindle, but whoever gathers little by little will increase it."**

Scripture warns us about sin —but also about speed.

In the Kingdom, **pace matters**.

Today's world is full of false shortcuts:

- "Instant crypto wealth"

- Empty forex promises

- Ponzi schemes disguised as "passive income"

- Online "experts" with no accountability

These schemes feed on impatience and desperation.

Even Jesus faced this temptation. In Matthew 4, Satan offered Him the kingdoms of the world **without the cross,** quick success without process. Jesus refused.

Gehazi chased wealth through deceit in 2 Kings 5. He ended up with leprosy not luxury.

If someone promises:

- "Huge returns fast,"

- "No work required,"

- "Guaranteed profits,"

Stop. Test it. Ask:

- Does it follow wisdom?

- Can you explain it simply?

- Does it create peace when you pray?

- Is it built on principle or hype?

The Kingdom operates on **seed → time → harvest.**

Time is not the enemy. It is the protection. Time builds character and discernment.

If it bypasses integrity, it is not God.

If it bypasses process, it won't last.

If it bypasses accountability, it is dangerous.

You don't need hype. You need wisdom.

Real wealth grows with consistency, excellence, and patience.

Emotional Spending and Impulse Buying

Emotional spending hides behind the illusion of reward but leaves the sting of regret. It's the swipe that soothes stress, the click that calms comparison, the package that feels like control… until the bill arrives.

> *Proverbs 25:28 says, "A man without self-control is like a city broken into and left without walls." Every impulse purchase chips away your protection.*

Emotional spending is subtle. It shows up when:

- Stress is high

- Boredom whispers

- Insecurity wants approval

- Loneliness meets a Buy Now button

Retail therapy feels powerful, but trades long-term peace for short-term relief.

Payday splurges look like celebration but sabotage goals.

"I deserve this," becomes the most expensive sentence in your vocabulary.

Social media magnifies the trap. Every scroll brings a new "must-have," pushing you toward spending instead of your calling.

Freedom begins with awareness.

Track every dollar for 30 days. Patterns appear. Triggers surface. Emotion-fueled purchases become obvious.

Then install a **48-hour rule**:

Wait two days before buying anything non-essential.

If it still aligns with your purpose and budget, proceed.

If not, the emotion will likely fade.

Replace the trigger:

Journal. Walk. Pray. Call a mentor.

Shift the emotion before you swipe.

This isn't restriction, it's **redirection**.

Your financial destiny needs discipline. Emotional spending is not a money problem; it's a **mastery problem**.

Mastery says "no" today to build "yes" tomorrow.

Mastery chooses peace over plastic.

You're not led by your feelings. You're led by the Spirit.

Purpose, not emotion, should guide your money.

Your destiny is worth protecting

Beware of Comparison and Greed

Comparison has a quiet voice but a loud impact. It often whispers when no one sees you winning. When someone else gets the promotion. When their house is bigger. When their business grows faster. If left unchecked, comparison becomes a thief. It steals contentment, clouds purpose, and corrupts stewardship.

Jesus warned in Luke 12:15, "Watch out! Be on your guard against all kinds of greed; life does not consist in an abundance of possessions." Greed doesn't always look extreme. Sometimes it shows up as a subtle disappointment when someone else succeeds.

Comparison breeds insecurity. It causes overspending, not because you need more, but because you're trying to **look** like more. It pushes you to chase time-lines, promotions, and purchases that God never assigned to you.

Cain killed Abel because he compared his offering to his brother's. Abel didn't harm him, comparison did. In Luke 15, the elder brother stayed faithful in the house but missed the heart of the father. He stood outside the celebration, offended that his brother was honored. He thought he deserved more. Greed blinds you to grace.

Judas betrayed Jesus for silver. What looked like a financial decision was really a **value** decision. When greed leads, something sacred is always sacrificed.

The antidote is **radical gratitude and generosity**.

Take breaks from social media if it pushes you into performance. Celebrate the wins of others out loud, your turn is not canceled. It is being cultivated. Anchor your identity in calling, not competition. Purpose, not possessions, defines you.

Pause and write down three things you're grateful for today.

Declare this out loud:

- **"I don't chase things. I steward purpose.**

- **I celebrate what God is doing in others.**

- **I trust what He is doing in me."**

Contentment is not complacency. It is peace rooted in trust. It says, "I can grow without grinding outside of God's timing." It is not settling; it is standing strong while you wait.

Greed pushes you toward idols. Gratitude anchors you to the Kingdom. Comparison chokes clarity. Gratitude opens vision. The enemy of wealth isn't always lack; it's wanting what was never assigned to you.

Stay in your lane. Build what God gave you. Multiply what He entrusted to you.

That is where the reward is.

Wealth is not only something you build. It is something you guard. Many begin well but lose their progress through silent traps.

- Debt becomes slavery when unmanaged, but freedom is possible with structure and wisdom.

- Quick wealth offers shortcuts, but what is gained fast rarely lasts.

- Emotional spending steals peace and drains destiny.

- Comparison shifts your focus and pulls you off your assignment.

Avoiding these traps is not fear, it is wisdom. It is how Kingdom builders endure. Protecting the harvest is just as important as sowing the seed.

Ask yourself:

- **What needs pruning before promotion?**

- **What habits must end so increase can begin?**

This is not guilt. This is alignment.

You've now learned how to create, manage, and multiply. But none of it matters if the motive is lost. That is why the next chapter is critical. You are not called to get rich so you can get comfortable.

> You are called to prosper so that others can flourish through you.

In the next chapter, we'll explore **why God wants to prosper you** and how your increase fuels Kingdom impact.

13

PURPOSE-DRIVEN INVESTING

"When purpose is not known, abuse is inevitable." —Myles Munroe

What would you do if ten million dollars hit your account today? How much would only serve your lifestyle, and how much would shape eternity? That question is not guilt, it's guidance. Wealth without purpose leads to self-centered living. But wealth with purpose becomes fuel for transformation.

God never blesses without intention. He increases you so His influence through you can expand. Purpose-driven wealth flows from stewardship, obedience, and vision. It carries peace because it is aligned with His Kingdom.

This chapter shifts your focus from accumulation to assignment. You are blessed to be a blessing. Money is a servant, not a master. And when your finances follow God's will, your impact multiplies beyond your own comfort.

You'll also learn how to give with clarity instead of emotion, structure generosity for long-term influence, and understand how your business, platform, or products can fund Kingdom work.

Whether you're a teacher, CEO, artist, parent, or entrepreneur, your wealth carries a divine assignment. You were never called to only consume; you are called to convert currency into influence. Let's explore how to fund Kingdom assignments, give with wisdom, and turn money into a megaphone for the Gospel.

Because you weren't born just to get rich. You were born to leave a legacy that echoes in eternity.

God Blesses You to Be a Blessing

The most dangerous thing about wealth is forgetting *why* God gave it to you. Accumulation without assignment leads to vanity. The Kingdom doesn't increase for ego, it increases for impact.

God told Abraham, *"I will bless you, and you will be a blessing"* (Genesis 12:2). The blessing was never meant to stop with him. It was meant to flow through him. That principle has not changed. You are not a vault; you are a vessel.

Proverbs 11:25 says, *"A generous person will prosper; whoever refreshes others will be refreshed."* What you release multiplies. What you hoard decays. Heaven looks for distribution centers, not collectors.

Wealth in the Kingdom carries a covenant assignment. God increases people to fulfill divine responsibility, funding families, ministries, justice work, and mercy assignments. When He finds someone who keeps the river flowing, He enlarges the stream.

Purpose-anchored giving produces joy. You begin to ask better questions:

- What lives am I lifting?

- What burdens am I lightening?

- What impact am I funding?

- What injustice am I confronting?

Review your current giving. Where does your money flow? Do you track generosity as seriously as you track income? Giving reflects priorities. What does your generosity say about your purpose?

Ask yourself: *"Who am I consistently blessing?"* Not once, but consistently. Someone is depending on your obedience. Your finances were not meant to build monuments to your success. They were meant to build Kingdom impact through your surrender.

Wealth that flows through you becomes legacy. It builds houses for widows, schools for children, and churches in unreached places. It turns money into ministry. God doesn't need you to be rich, He needs you to be ready. Ready to say yes. Ready to meet needs. Ready to fund assignment.

A blessed life is not the goal. A blessing in life is the goal.

When you live as a blessing, increase follows you without strain. God fills what He can trust. You were blessed for more than bills and brunch. You were blessed to be a bridge between what Heaven has and what Earth lacks.

Funding Kingdom Assignments

Money is not the destination, it is transportation. Without assignment, wealth has noise but no melody. With assignment, it becomes revival fuel.

Luke 8:3 shows that women financially supported Jesus' ministry. Heaven's work required earthly resources. God used financially equipped people to back His mission.

Nehemiah rebuilt Jerusalem with prayer, boldness, and resources. Exodus 35 shows that the tabernacle was built through freewill offerings. Even divine projects required human generosity.

Margaret Thatcher once said, *"No one would have remembered the Good Samaritan if he'd only had good intentions; he had money as well."* Good intentions don't build impact. Resources do.

Kingdom assignments still need Kingdom backers. Missions require funding. Discipleship programs need materials. Orphanages need infrastructure. Justice work needs legal teams. Content creation needs equipment and distribution. God still funds His work through willing people.

If your heart burns for any ministry or cause, it may be calling. Maybe not to go, but to send. Money touches places your feet will never walk.

What if your finances were pre-assigned to Kingdom goals? What if you committed a percentage of increase to a mission God placed on your heart?

Ask:

- *What assignment has God placed on my heart?*

- *If money were no object, what would I fund?*

Purpose doesn't wait for wealth. It prepares for it.

When your finances align with God's blueprint, you don't just give, you become a Kingdom financier. Wealth with assignment becomes revival fuel. It doesn't just bring relief. It builds reformation.

God is raising financial reformers, people who pray with a spreadsheet and build with a Bible. The question isn't "How much can I make?" but "How much Kingdom can I build with what I've been given?"

Giving With Wisdom

Giving is powerful, but without direction it loses impact. Scripture calls for purposeful, Spirit-led generosity, not pressured or emotional giving.

Proverbs 3:9 says, *"Honor the Lord with your wealth..."*

2 Corinthians 9:7 says, *"Give what you have decided in your heart..."*

The most effective givers are not the most emotional. They're the most intentional. They pray, plan, and structure generosity the same way they steward businesses or families.

Wise giving includes categories with different purposes:

Tithes: The first 10% returned to the local church. Tithing is covenant alignment, not optional generosity.

Offerings: Seeds for ministry projects, mentors, missions, or faith assignments.

Alms: Compassion for the poor and hurting. This is mercy-giving, not investment-giving.

First Fruits: A special offering at the start of a new job, raise, or income stream. It honors God as first.

Legacy Giving

Scholarships, nonprofits, church plants, or long-term impact structures.

But wise giving also sets boundaries. Not every need is your assignment. Many believers are drained because they give from guilt, pressure, or manipulation. Toxic giving uses fear:

- "Prove your faith by this amount."

- "If you don't give, God won't bless you."

That's not Kingdom. That's control.

A simple giving portfolio brings structure:

- 40% Local church

- 30% Missions / church plants

- 20% Justice initiatives

- 10% Spontaneous generosity

You can adjust based on calling. The point is clarity.

Strategic giving multiplies your reach. Spirit-led generosity is spiritual warfare. It moves mountains and builds what emotion cannot sustain.

Wealth as a Tool for Evangelism

Wealth has a voice. It can whisper self-indulgence or shout Kingdom truth. When aligned with God, money becomes more than provision, it becomes proclamation.

Luke 16:9 reveals the eternal power of financial stewardship. Money, used well, impacts eternity. Zechariah 1:17 confirms that God's cities spread out through prosperity. Kingdom wealth advances Kingdom purpose.

Every evangelism initiative requires funding, Bible translation, church plants, media outreach, youth discipleship, crusades, humanitarian work. Kingdom wealth is not about building castles, it's about launching campaigns for souls.

The Good Samaritan didn't just pray. He paid. His compassion turned into contribution.

Modern believers are doing the same:

- Businesses tithing revenue

- Creatives funding Bible translation

- Entrepreneurs building digital discipleship

- Small businesses underwriting missionaries

You don't need a pulpit to preach. You only need to partner.

Ask yourself:

- If God increased me tenfold, would my giving increase too?

- Would the Gospel go farther because I had more?

If the answer is yes, then your increase is mission ready.

Your money is a messenger. Aim it well.

Declare: ***"My money is a message. I fund Kingdom influence. I build altars, not idols."***

You are not storing for storage's sake. You are blessed to be a blessing. Wealth with purpose multiplies into eternal impact.

Wealth without purpose breeds pride. But wealth tied to Kingdom assignment multiplies into eternity. Strategic giving is spiritual warfare. God is looking for people He can trust with more, so they can *do* more.

Your money is not just currency. It's a messenger.

In the next chapter, we move from purpose to inheritance, how to pass on faith, values, and wealth to build Kingdom legacy across generations.

14

LEGACY: BUILDING WEALTH ACROSS GENERATIONS

"A good man leaves an inheritance to his children's children."
—Proverbs 13:22 (NKJV)

What if everything you're building dies with you? What if your income stops, your influence fades, and your wealth disappears because you never planned for who comes after you?

This is the story of many families. Money is earned and lost in one generation, not because wealth was bad, but because succession was missing.

> **Kingdom wealth always thinks in generations.** It builds beyond one lifetime. It plans for impact that continues after you're gone.

This chapter is not only about preserving dollars. It's about preserving **decisions, values, and vision**. Generational wealth is more than a trust fund. It is a **God-trust**, the intentional transfer of truth, stewardship, structure, and spiritual legacy.

Wealth without succession dies quickly. Wealth handed down with wisdom builds Kingdom infrastructure for decades.

Your legacy is not built on what you consume, **it's built on what you transfer.**

Here's what this chapter will help you do:

- See why leaving an inheritance is biblical and strategic

- Teach your children about wealth through a Kingdom lens

- Protect what you build with legal and practical structures

- Understand why mentorship is essential for legacy

You are not only called to **build wealth.**

You are called to **leave a legacy that multiplies.**

A Good Man Leaves an Inheritance
Proverbs 13:22

"A good man leaves an inheritance to his children's children..." —Proverbs 13:22

If what you're building ends with you, it wasn't legacy, only maintenance.

Scripture is clear: the righteous think *generationally*. Not only about their children, but about their **children's children**.

A good man plans beyond his lifetime. His wealth sustains his home and positions his lineage for Kingdom impact.

Inheritance includes more than money. It includes:

- Systems

- Mindsets

- Disciplines

- Convictions

- Tangible assets (property, businesses, investments)

- Intangible assets (faith, integrity, work ethic, spiritual discernment)

Abraham passed down more than livestock, he passed down a **covenant**.

David stored up resources and plans so Solomon could build the temple.

God calls Himself the God of Abraham, Isaac, and Jacob because His covenant moves generationally.

Our culture glorifies consuming everything now.

Kingdom wealth builders ask deeper questions:

- What am I passing down with my money?

- Am I equipping my children, or enabling them?

- Will they inherit wisdom, or confusion?

You are not called to die wealthy.

You are called to pass the baton and **die empty, having poured out wisdom, values, and faith.**

This starts now, not at age 80. Every financial choice today shapes someone's tomorrow.

> Ask yourself:
>
> *"Am I building something my grandchildren can benefit from, or something only I can enjoy?"*

Teaching Your Children About Wealth

"Train up a child…" —Proverbs 22:6

"Teach them diligently…" —Deuteronomy 6:6–7

Wealth transfer begins long before wills are written.

Children don't inherit wisdom by accident. They inherit what's taught, explained, and modeled.

Too many families leave money without mindset. That creates entitlement, not legacy.

Start early. Even young children can learn stewardship:

- Give them a simple allowance

- Teach them to divide it (spend, save, give)

- Talk about **why**, not just **how**

- Show them how money has purpose, not just pleasure

Let them see real examples:

- Your tithe

- Your giving goals

- How you save for a project

- How you pray over financial decisions

Normalize stewardship as a lifestyle.

Make generosity a family culture:

- Choose a giving project together

- Support a missionary or a local outreach

- Help a family in need

These moments stick deeper than lectures.

Build simple tools:

- A family wealth confession ("We are stewards, not owners...")

- A weekly principle ("This is why we save...")

Children need **presence and mentorship**, not perfection. When they see you live with purpose, they learn to carry purpose.

> **Your children are arrows. Wealth is the bow. Shape them well.**

Estate Planning and Legacy Documents

"The prudent see danger and take refuge..." —Proverbs 27:12

Estate planning is not about death. It's about **order, stewardship, and love**.

Many families lose wealth, not because they lacked money, but because they lacked preparation. Without clarity, families end up in:

- Court battles

- Confusion

- Delays

- Lost assets

Estate planning is prophetic stewardship. It says:

"The vision will not stop with me."

Every believer with children, assets, or financial responsibility needs a plan.

Core documents include:

- **Will** – Directs how your assets are distributed

- **Living Trust** – Avoids probate and allows smoother transfer

- **Healthcare Directive** – States your medical decisions

- **Power of Attorney** – Appoints someone to act for you

- **Beneficiary Designations** – Ensures accounts go to the right people

These documents create clarity, protect relationships, and keep your financial legacy aligned with your values.

Don't DIY your estate. Seek a Christian financial advisor or estate attorney.

Estate planning is your **final financial sermon**.

Let it speak with clarity, honor, and Kingdom purpose.

Mentorship and Wealth Transfer

"And what you have heard from me... entrust to faithful men..." —2 Timothy 2:2

Assets alone don't create legacy, **mentorship does**.

Wealth without discipleship produces entitled heirs.

Wealth with discipleship produces Kingdom stewards.

Moses prepared Joshua.

Elijah prepared Elisha.

Jesus prepared the disciples.

Before handing over anything, they imparted:

- Character

- Vision

- Habits

- Courage

- Spiritual authority

This is true wealth transfer.

Mentorship includes:

- Regular conversations

- Guided decisions

- Sharing wisdom and mistakes

- Teaching values, not just numbers

A "Wealth Legacy Plan" is more than instructions, it is direction, principles, and purpose.

Pray over your successors. Speak over them. Walk with them. Show them how to multiply what you built.

Legacy is not about leaving something behind.

It's about **launching someone forward.**

You are not just a wealth builder.

You are a legacy maker.

Let generations rise and call you blessed, not just because of what you gave them, but because of what you taught them to carry.

PART 2

THE LAWS OF WEALTH

15

THE LAW OF ABUNDANCE: GOD'S UNLIMITED SUPPLY

*"Write the vision and make it plain on tablets, that he may run who reads it."— **Habakkuk 2:2 (NKJV)***

Have you ever wondered why some people expect more out of life, while others seem convinced there is never enough to go around? This mindset shapes every decision you make, from how you spend money to the way you view opportunity. **The Law of Abundance** begins with a truth that can feel almost surprising: God created a world filled with plenty. Most people do not struggle because the world has run out. They struggle because they have learned to see limits everywhere.

If you would like a deeper foundation on this shift from scarcity to Kingdom abundance, return to Part 1. There you will find the core principles that prepare your heart and mind for what this chapter builds upon.

Jesus affirmed this in John 10:10 (NKJV): "I have come that they may have life, and that they may have it more abundantly."

Abundance is not a distant promise. It is the kind of life Jesus offers today, a life marked by provision, peace, and sufficiency in every season.

David echoes the same truth. *"The Lord is my shepherd; I shall not want."* (Psalm 23:1, NKJV). This is not simply a comforting verse. It is a declaration of God's consistent supply. His care reaches every area of your life, and His provision exceeds every shortage.

Scarcity thinking whispers, *"There is not enough."* It shows up as fear, anxiety, and tight-fisted living.

Children argue over snacks, adults worry about layoffs, and businesses shrink during uncertainty. Scarcity causes people to protect what they have, afraid that it will disappear.

Abundance tells a different story. It says, *"God's supply is greater than any need."* This mindset produces generosity, creativity, and courage. People who believe in abundance notice possibilities others overlook. They collaborate freely and celebrate the success of others because they understand that blessing multiplies.

The Law of Abundance teaches that when you truly see God as your limitless Source, opportunities begin to appear even in difficult times. This principle challenges you to examine how you view the world and how you view yourself. Fear loses its power when you are convinced that God is providing for you. Even when the numbers look tight or the news seems discouraging, faith keeps you looking for ways to give, build, and move forward.

God wants you to see abundance where others see lack. The next time you hear yourself think, *"There is not enough,"* ask what would shift if you genuinely believed God's supply never ends. This transformation changes more than your finances. It changes the way you live.

Stories of Abundance from Scripture and Today

Sometimes it takes a crisis to reveal what we truly believe about God's ability to provide. In 2 Kings 7, Israel faced a famine so severe that hope was nearly gone. Food was scarce, prices had soared, and fear had settled over the nation. In the middle of this crisis, the prophet Elisha spoke a promise from God: within twenty-four hours, food would be plentiful again. Although no one saw a possible solution, God was already at work.

The narrative then turns to four men with leprosy who sat outside the city gate. They had every reason to give up, yet they asked a bold question: "*Why sit here until we die?*" Instead of waiting for rescue, they moved toward the enemy camp. When they arrived, they discovered that God had caused the enemy to flee. The camp was filled with food, silver, and supplies. Their simple step opened the door to the miracle the city needed. Abundance arrived because faith moved forward.

A similar principle appears in everyday life. Consider a father who worked faithfully for fifteen years until his company closed during a recession. Bills continued to arrive, but instead of freezing in fear, he took an inventory of his skills. With only a pickup truck and a few tools, he offered handyman services to his neighbors. Small tasks soon led to steady work, and eventually his small effort grew into a stable source of income. He discovered new provision because he moved in faith instead of waiting in fear.

Another example comes from a mother whose hours were reduced at work. She loved baking and decided to make a batch of cookies for friends. Their response inspired her to post a few photos online. Orders came in quickly, and before long she was supplying birthday treats and celebration cakes. What began as a temporary effort became a thriving business that provided for her home and gave her a way to bless others.

What do these stories share? People who trust God for abundance look for doors where others see walls. When fear says stop, faith says take a step. When one source closes, creativity makes room for another. You may not control every circumstance, but you can control how you respond.

The lesson remains the same across every generation. Abundance is not only what you hold in your hand. It is what fills your heart and directs your mindset. God's supply reaches those who move forward with courage, vision, and expectation.

How to Practice Abundance Mindset

Your mindset is the lens through which you see every opportunity, challenge, or setback. People who expect abundance look for ways to grow and give, even when their circumstances appear limited. You can train your mind to spot open doors, not just barriers, no matter what season you are in.

Start with your words. When you hear yourself say, "I can't afford that," try shifting to, "How can I create or receive what I need?" Speaking life over your situation makes a difference. Read Psalm 23:1 out loud each morning: "The Lord is my shepherd; I shall not want." This daily reminder centers you on God as your source and provider.

Opportunities do not always announce themselves. Instead, ask, "What new need can I serve?" Maybe a neighbor needs help with a small task, or your workplace faces a new challenge. Recall the lepers from 2 Kings 7. They took a step forward when fear told them to freeze. Their willingness to act led to an outcome no one expected.

Celebrate the success of others. Jealousy keeps your heart closed. Abundance grows when you can cheer someone else's breakthrough. If a friend gets promoted, or a family member launches a business, celebrate. Gratitude multiplies what you have.

Even when you feel stretched, choose generosity. Give time, share a meal, or encourage someone. Generosity creates new streams of blessing, even when the resources seem small.

You can start today with these simple shifts:

- Replace lack-focused language with questions of faith and possibility.

- Watch for needs around you, no matter how small.

- Speak God's promises aloud.

- Find ways to celebrate others' progress.

- Share, even when you feel limited.

Reflection: Where have you been thinking *"not enough"*? What could happen if you trusted God's abundance instead?

John 10:10 says, *"I have come that they may have life, and that they may have it more abundantly."* Psalm 23:1 reminds you, "The Lord is my shepherd; I shall not want." God's plan for you is overflowing life. Your mindset opens the door to receive it.

16

THE LAW OF INVESTMENT: MULTIPLYING WHAT YOU'VE BEEN GIVEN

Every successful harvest started with a single seed. The secret is not just to work hard, but to work wisely and invest what you have. The Law of Investment is straightforward: ***when you have money and you do not invest it, it does not grow. Your portfolio will never grow unless you invest.*** What you invest, your time, money, or energy, can grow and multiply, creating a future harvest.

Investment is about more than opening a bank account or buying stocks. Every choice to grow, help, or build is a form of investment. Think about planting a garden. It begins with one seed, a little care each day, and over time, the seed produces fruit. Starting a savings jar, spending a few minutes each night learning a new skill, or reaching out to help a neighbor all count as investments. You decide what grows in your life by what you are willing to plant.

This principle is rooted in scripture. In Matthew 25:14–30 (NKJV), Jesus shares the Parable of the Talents. A master gives three servants different amounts of money and leaves them to manage it. Two of the servants invest what they are given, doubling their share. The third buries his talent, afraid of losing it. When the master returns, he rewards the investors and calls out the one who hid his gift. The message is clear: God expects you to use what you have, not to hoard it, but to make it grow for His purposes.

Investment includes money, but it goes far beyond that. Your time spent learning, your willingness to help someone, your energy used to build a project, or nurture a friendship, these are seeds. Each one holds potential for multiplication if you sow them faithfully.

You do not need a large sum or special qualifications to start. Anyone can be an investor. The smallest effort, repeated with wisdom and consistency, adds up. Even one coin in a jar, one hour reading, or one act of kindness can create a harvest down the line.

> God honors those who invest what they have. Growth always begins with a seed you are willing to plant today.

Investment in Action

Some of the most powerful breakthroughs in life start with one small investment. In Matthew 25:14–30, Jesus tells the story of a master who entrusts three servants with different amounts of money, called talents. Two of them invest and double what they receive. The third, gripped by fear, buries his talent, and returns only what he was given. When the master returns, he praises the investors and rewards their effort. The servant who played it safe misses out, losing even the small portion he started with.

The lesson stands out clearly: God takes pleasure when you grow and multiply what He places in your hands. Hiding your skills, waiting for perfect conditions, or holding back out of fear only limits your potential. The law is not about perfection, but about movement, using and growing what you have.

Everyday life is full of similar stories. Think of a woman who begins saving one dollar a day, even while living on a tight budget. Over time, her discipline grows into a solid emergency fund. That fund becomes seed money for a small business she starts from home. Her steady investment in herself brings her new skills, greater confidence, and a new stream of income.

Look at the young man who volunteers at a local community center. He helps with events, supports after-school programs, and builds trust with staff. Months later, when a paid position opens, his commitment and attitude make him the natural choice. Investing effort and reliability pays off, turning service into opportunity.

A father of three puts aside thirty minutes a day to learn Spanish using a free app. After a year, he speaks fluently enough to take on new responsibilities at work. His investment in learning brings a raise and opens doors to travel with his company.

What do these stories reveal?

- Small, steady investments grow into big results over time.

- Effort given in relationships, learning, or serving always produces fruit in the future.

- Opportunities find those who prepare and invest, even in simple ways.

Each step you take, saving, serving, building skills, counts as an investment. The breakthrough you need tomorrow begins with the seed you are willing to plant today. Keep investing, and let God multiply what you faithfully steward.

How to Start Investing

Big results come from small steps repeated with intention. Investing is not just for the wealthy or experienced; it starts with everyday choices that add up over time. You can begin right where you are, no matter how much or how little you have.

Start with money. Open a simple savings account and put away a little each week. Even a few coins or small bills, set aside regularly, will build a habit, and create a foundation for the future. If you are ready, explore basic, low-risk investments. Always seek wise counsel and financial advice when you try something new.

Invest your time. Block a short window each day or week for personal growth, reading a book, practicing a new skill, or taking a free online course. Make time for people who inspire you or can help you grow, whether it is a call with a mentor or a walk with a wise friend.

Invest in your relationships. Offer encouragement, share advice, or help someone with a project. A kind word, a helping hand, or genuine support sown today can multiply back to you in unexpected ways.

Keep track of what you invest. Use a simple notebook to record your progress, how much you save, what you learn, or who you help. Review your notes often to see how your small actions are already producing growth.

Pause and ask yourself: What is one small way you can invest today, in your finances, your learning, or your relationships? Write it down and commit to doing it this week.

Great things start small. God honors faithful stewards who are willing to invest what they have, right now. Every step you take sows the seed for a harvest ahead.

17

THE LAW OF COMPOUND INTEREST: THE SILENT WEALTH ACCELERATOR

"Wealth gained by dishonesty will be diminished, but he who gathers by labor will increase."— **Proverbs 13:11 (NKJV)**

Have you ever wondered how small, daily choices can become a fortune over time? The answer is simple and powerful: compound interest. This law is not just for experts or people with big bank accounts. It is available to anyone willing to grow what they have, step by step.

The Law of Compound Interest states: Wealth grows fastest when what you earn starts to earn more for you, over and over, little by little. Compound interest works like a snowball rolling down a hill, what starts small gains speed and size with every turn. When you save or invest a little each week, those small amounts add up. Over time, the interest or growth you earn is added to your original sum. Soon, your savings start to earn their own returns. This cycle repeats, multiplying what you started with.

Scripture anchors this principle in Proverbs 13:11 (NKJV): "Wealth gained by dishonesty will be diminished, but he who gathers by labor will increase." God's way is honest, steady growth, not chasing fast money or quick schemes. Consistency and patience are what bring real increase.

Many people dream of a big win, but compound interest rewards the faithful with steady growth. You do not need a lot to start, just a decision and a small, regular habit. Whether you are saving pocket change, investing five dollars a week, or building a new skill day by day, the power comes from doing it again and again. The results build on themselves until what was once small becomes something much greater.

Anyone can benefit from this law, no matter the size of their paycheck. Every dollar, every step, and every wise choice compounds for your future. Start small and let your little by little become much.

Compound Interest in Action

Most people wish for a financial breakthrough, but few realize how steady, honest growth transforms small choices into lasting wealth. Proverbs 13:11 (NKJV) says, "Wealth gained by dishonesty will be diminished, but he who gathers by labor will increase." God's plan rewards consistency over quick shortcuts.

Start with the simple example of saving one dollar a day. After a year, you have three hundred sixty-five dollars. Now put that money in a savings account with interest. Each month, not only do you add more dollars, but your interest earns more interest. The total starts growing on its own, even while you sleep. The small steps repeat until you look up and see your money multiplying beyond what you started with.

Picture planting an apple seed in your backyard. After a few seasons, the seed becomes a tree. That tree produces apples, and every apple holds more seeds. When you plant those seeds, your single tree turns into an orchard. That is how compound interest works. What you build in the beginning becomes the foundation for greater results down the line.

A real story brings this home. A teenager named Ben started saving ten dollars a week from his part-time job. He stuck to his plan for five years, putting his money into an account that paid interest. As his savings grew, the interest earned each month got bigger. Years later, Ben's friends tried to catch up by saving large chunks at once, but the person who started small and stayed consistent saw his money multiply the most.

This principle goes far beyond money. Think of a musician who spends fifteen minutes a day practicing piano. Those minutes add up over months and years. The skill grows, confidence builds, and opportunities appear. A little invested regularly compounds into a life-changing result.

Key points to remember:

- Saving or investing small amounts, often, creates real growth.

- Time and consistency are more important than big, one-time actions.

- Compound interest also applies to skills, relationships, and health.

> Little by little really does make a lot. Your commitment to steady, honest growth will always pay off in the long run.

How to Use Compound Interest

You do not need a big windfall to start benefiting from compound interest. The real key is to begin now and build a habit you can stick with, no matter how small.

Start small and start now. Open a savings account, even if you can only put away one dollar this week. If you feel ready, look into simple investments. The amount matters far less than your commitment to consistency. Small deposits, made regularly, grow over time.

Reinvest your returns. Each time you receive interest or make a profit, put it back to work. Avoid spending your gains right away. When your money earns more money, and you keep it in the account, growth speeds up. Your savings or investments begin to multiply on their own.

Be patient. Compound interest grows slowly in the beginning. Trust the process. Over months and years, the results become clear. Remember what Proverbs 13:11 (NKJV) says: "He who gathers by labor will increase." Your diligence is building something real.

Track your growth. Use a notebook or an app to write down your savings or investment progress every month. Watching the numbers rise, even little by little, will motivate you to keep going.

Ask yourself, what small step can you take today to start your compound journey? Could you save one, five, or ten dollars a week? How could you reinvest what you earn or learn for even greater growth?

God honors faithfulness in small things. Let your little by little become much, and your future self will thank you. Each step you take today will multiply into greater blessing tomorrow.

18

THE LAW OF MULTIPLE STREAMS: DESIGNING DIVERSIFIED INCOME

"Give a serving to seven, and also to eight, for you do not know what evil will be on the earth."— *Ecclesiastes 11:2 (NKJV)*

What happens if your only source of income dries up? For many, crisis begins not because of a lack of skill or work ethic, but because their options are limited to just one paycheck or business. The Law of Multiple Income Streams is clear: Relying on only one way to earn money is risky, multiple streams mean stability and growth.

This wisdom is not just modern advice; it is firmly rooted in the Bible. In 2 Kings 4, a widow faced overwhelming debt after her husband's death. God's solution, spoken through the prophet Elisha, was not a one-time miracle but a practical, repeatable system: gather as many empty jars as possible, pour out her oil, and sell it. The oil kept flowing as long as there were vessels. Many jars, many streams. This principle shows God values preparation and resourcefulness.

Ecclesiastes 11:2 (NKJV) echoes this idea: "Give a serving to seven, and also to eight, for you do not know what evil will be on the earth." One field may fail, but a wise farmer plant several. One river may dry up, but a lake fed by many rivers stays full. Depending on a single paycheck, client, or business makes your financial life fragile. Multiple income streams provide both a safety net and a springboard for new opportunities.

This law does not require you to become a business expert or risk everything. Anyone can add a stream, no matter where they start. Having several sources of income is not about greed, it is about wisdom and stewardship. With each additional stream, you increase your protection and your potential. God honors those who prepare and diversify, providing more than one way for His blessing to reach you.

Multiple Streams in Scripture and Everyday Life

In the Bible, God often provided for His people in more than one way. The widow in 2 Kings 4 did not stop with a single jar or one sale. Each new vessel meant another stream of income. Her story is a model for building stability in uncertain times. Another scripture, Proverbs 21:20 (NKJV), reinforces this approach: "There is desirable treasure, and oil in the dwelling of the wise, but a foolish man squanders it." Wise people not only save but also look for opportunities to add to what they have.

Depending on just one source puts you at risk. If your only client leaves or your employer cuts hours, bills still come due. Scripture and common sense say: spread your efforts, diversify your sources, and plan for the unexpected.

This wisdom applies to modern life in countless ways:

Part-time work:

A teacher drives a ride-share on weekends to pay down debt faster. A nurse knits and sells scarves at a holiday market. These second incomes may start small, but they add valuable security.

Small business or side hustle:

Many people bake goods, mow lawns, clean houses, or sell items online. These activities can supplement a main job and sometimes grow into something bigger. One dad started cleaning offices after work. That side job became his family's main business.

Digital skills:

A college student freelances as a graphic designer in the evenings, picking up projects online. A mom uses her writing talent to create blog content for companies around the world. Technology makes it easier than ever to start a second- or third-income stream from home.

Family model:

Even households with a steady main provider benefit from extra income. A stay-at-home parent sells crafts, or a teen helps with local yard work during school breaks. Every bit adds up and makes the family less vulnerable to job loss or surprise expenses.

Multiple streams bring peace of mind. If one dries up or slows down, another can help carry you through tough months. The goal is not to work yourself to exhaustion, but to wisely use your time, skills, and resources. When you spread your efforts, you open more doors for God's blessing and build a strong, resilient financial future.

Practical Steps to Build More Streams

Building multiple streams of income starts right where you are. Begin with what you know. Make a quick list of your skills, hobbies, or the things people ask you for help with most. Ask yourself, "What do people say I'm good at?" Your natural strengths might be the seed for a new stream.

Look for small opportunities close to home. Could you tutor a student, sell crafts online, walk dogs, help with events, or take on digital jobs like editing or virtual assistance? Sometimes, the simplest idea is right in front of you, a neighbor needing help, a friend looking for a part-time worker, or a local event needing extra hands.

Tap into your network. Reach out to family, friends, church, or even your social media contacts. Let people know what you can offer and ask if they know anyone who needs those skills. Many side incomes start with one word-of-mouth connection.

Pick one new stream to try this month. Keep it small and manageable. The goal is to build confidence, not to overwhelm yourself. Track your results and adjust as you learn what works best for you.

Never stop learning. Invest in a basic course, attend a workshop, or read about ways to improve your new skill or side business. Every bit of knowledge adds value to your efforts.

> What's one small way you could earn an extra $20, $50, or $100 this month? Write it down, pray for God's wisdom, and take that first step.

Every extra stream is both a blessing and a buffer. Success does not depend on how big you start, but that you start. Each new effort gives God more room to multiply your increase.

19

THE LAW OF SAVING: PRESERVING SEED FOR YOUR FUTURE

"There is desirable treasure, and oil in the dwelling of the wise, but a foolish man squanders it."— Proverbs 21:20 (NKJV)

Have you ever felt a twinge of guilt setting aside money, wondering if saving means you lack faith in God's provision? Many believers wrestle with this, but what if saving is not a sign of fear, it is actually a mark of godly wisdom? The Law of Saving teaches that saving is not just good sense, it is spiritual wisdom and a way to honor God with your resources.

Scripture speaks directly to this principle. Proverbs 21:20 (NKJV) says, "There is desirable treasure, and oil in the dwelling of the wise, but a foolish man squanders it." Wise people prepare and store; those who waste live with constant pressure and regret. Saving is not about being selfish or greedy. It means planning ahead, protecting your family, and creating a margin so you can give, invest, or respond to life's emergencies without panic.

Some people confuse saving with hoarding, but the two are very different. Hoarding is rooted in fear and an unhealthy need to control. Saving is stewardship, putting aside a portion of what you have so you are ready for both opportunities and unexpected needs. God never called you to live recklessly or hand-to-mouth if you have any way to plan ahead.

Saving is practical at every income level. If you only have a small paycheck, start with coins in a jar or a small bill tucked away from each payday. If you have more, commit a percentage before you do anything else. This habit not only protects you from future stress but frees you to be generous and invest in others when the need arises.

It does not matter if you have struggled with saving before. Today is a new chance to start. God honors even your smallest steps of wisdom and discipline. You do not need a large sum, just a willing heart and a plan. Begin with what you have, trust God for increase, and watch as saving brings peace, freedom, and strength to your financial life.

Saving in Scripture and Real Life

Think back to the story of Joseph in Egypt. Pharaoh had two dreams about seven years of plenty and seven years of famine. Joseph, guided by God's wisdom, advised Pharaoh to save a portion of Egypt's harvest during the good years. Grain was gathered, stored, and guarded while the land overflowed. When famine struck, Egypt had more than enough to feed its people and to help neighboring nations.

Joseph's approach did not focus on fear, but on faith-filled strategy. He understood that abundance in one season was meant to prepare for the lean times ahead. Egypt not only survived the crisis, but they also thrived, while others struggled. God's people became a source of hope and supply to the world because they saved when they could. This is the heart of Proverbs 21:20 (NKJV): "There is desirable treasure, and oil in the dwelling of the wise, but a foolish man squanders it." Saving brings peace, security, and options that wastefulness never offers.

You do not need a palace or a high-paying job to follow Joseph's wisdom. Meet Sarah, a single mother earning a modest wage. She began dropping spare coins into a jar each week, even when it felt like barely enough. Over time, her jar filled, and her habit grew stronger. One month, her son needed urgent medication, and the emergency fund she built saved the day. Sarah did not need to borrow or panic, her small, consistent saving created peace of mind and real provision.

Contrast that with James, who always spent his entire paycheck as soon as he received it. When his car broke down unexpectedly, he had no backup plan and ended up in debt. The stress and worry were constant companions because he lived without a margin.

Saving is not about the amount; it is the discipline and foresight that matter most. Whether you set aside five dollars or fifty, you are training yourself to honor God's wisdom. Even a simple coin jar or an envelope marked "savings" can be a game changer.

Key points to remember:

- Saving helps you weather life's storms with confidence.

- You bless others when you have something set aside.

- Even small amounts, saved regularly, can cover emergencies and open doors for generosity.

The stories of Joseph and Sarah show that anyone can build a habit of saving, no matter their season of life. It starts with honoring God's word, making a simple plan, and trusting Him to multiply your diligence. Saving today is not about fear, it is a gift to your future self and a testimony of wisdom to those around you.

How to Start Saving

Starting a habit of saving does not require a large income or a perfect plan. The key is to take the first step, no matter how small. Consistency wins over size every time. Even if you have never saved before, you can begin today, right where you are.

Start with a simple decision: set aside a fixed amount from every bit of income you receive. It could be just a few coins, a small bill, or a specific percentage that feels doable. The important part is to create a pattern that fits your reality. The act of saving, not the amount, is what sets your future in motion.

Treat your savings like a bill that must be paid. When you receive your paycheck or any money, move your chosen amount into a savings envelope, jar, or separate bank account before spending anything else. Paying yourself first puts saving at the top of your priorities. It means you value your future and trust God's wisdom in Proverbs 21:20 (NKJV): "There is desirable treasure, and oil in the dwelling of the wise, but a foolish man squanders it."

If you keep cash, label an envelope or a jar as "Savings." Make it a habit to drop in coins, loose change, or a set note each week. When you see it fill up, you build momentum. For those with bank accounts, take advantage of technology by setting up an automatic transfer to savings as soon as you are paid. Automation helps you stick with your plan, even on busy or difficult days.

As your savings grow, celebrate each milestone. Give thanks to God for every bit, no matter how small. Let gratitude strengthen your motivation and help you see each deposit as a seed for tomorrow's harvest. With every step, you move from worry to wisdom, from lack to margin.

Pause for a moment: What is one small thing you could give up or reduce this week to start saving? Maybe a daily snack, a subscription, or a minor expense. How much could you set aside, even if it feels tiny at first?

> Every small deposit counts. Small savings today are seeds for tomorrow's harvest.

God honors your wisdom and diligence. Your faithfulness in this area will open new possibilities for generosity, security, and peace. Start now, no matter where you are, and let your savings tell the story of your trust and discipline.

20

❦

THE LAW OF PATIENCE: THE WAITING THAT BUILDS WEALTH

"See how the farmer waits for the precious fruit of the earth, waiting patiently for it..."—James 5:7 (NKJV)

Have you ever planted a seed and hoped for fruit the next day? True growth demands patience. The Law of Patience works in the field, in your finances, and in your spirit. Wealth and blessing take time, what you plant today grows with patience and faith, not overnight. Many dreams die not because the seed is bad, but because patience runs out before the harvest can come.

Patience does not mean sitting on your hands and waiting for magic. Patience means trusting God and doing what you can, even when results seem slow. The farmer plants, waters, weeds, and watches, expecting fruit in due season. You save, give, learn, and pray, even if it feels like nothing is changing. Your faithful steps are never wasted.

When you try to force results, you can uproot what God is growing. Some people abandon a good habit, a business idea, or a savings plan because it takes longer than they hoped. Quick fixes may look tempting, but they often destroy what steady patience could have multiplied. Waiting well brings a better reward, one that lasts.

God built growth into seasons. The richest fields require time: rain must fall, roots must deepen, the sun must rise and set many times before harvest comes. Your life, your wealth, your dreams also unfold in seasons. Feeling "behind" or comparing yourself to others will only steal your peace.

This truth is echoed even in the world of investing. When Warren Buffett was asked, *"Why do people not emulate your style of investment?"* he replied, *"Because people do not have the patience to wait."* Long-term success often belongs to those willing to endure delay, volatility, and uncertainty.

Take a breath. Your progress is real, even when it is not visible yet. The Law of Patience is God's wisdom for those who trust the process. He promises in James 5:8: "Establish your hearts, for the coming of the Lord is at hand." That means steady your mind, anchor your hope, and keep moving forward. The harvest will come, in its appointed time.

Patience is strength, not weakness. It is active faith, not passive waiting. While you work, trust, and wait, God is working beneath the surface, multiplying what you have planted. This is your encouragement: what you start with patience, you will finish with joy.

Patience in Action

Patience sounds simple until you must live it. A farmer rises early, digs the ground, plants seeds, and watches the weather. There are weeks of watering, pulling weeds, and checking for signs of life. Still, no fruit appears overnight. The farmer trusts that beneath the soil, something good is happening. He does not dig up his seeds to see if they are sprouting. He trusts the process and keeps working, knowing the harvest comes only after the early and latter rains.

Scripture gives this vivid picture in James 5:7–8. *"See how the farmer waits for the precious fruit of the earth, waiting patiently for it until it receives the early and latter rain."* God built growth into seasons, there are planting days, waiting days, and finally, harvesting days. Farmers are patient by necessity. They cannot force fruit. They prepare, pray, and work, confident the earth will yield in due time.

Financial patience follows the same path. Even the most successful investors understand this. *Charlie Munger once said that you must be willing to lose as much as 50 percent of your portfolio if you want to get rich.* That statement shocks many people, but it reveals a deeper truth: real growth requires endurance, emotional discipline, and the patience to stay the course during downturns.

Take the story of a young woman starting her first job with a modest paycheck. Each week, she sets aside a small amount, sometimes just a handful of coins. After months, her savings are slow to grow, but she stays consistent. Over years, those tiny deposits build into a solid emergency fund. Patience gives her peace and provision when she needs it most.

Answered prayers often teach patience as well. A couple praying for a child learns that waiting seasons can deepen faith and strengthen character. When the answer comes, they realize the wait prepared them for the blessing.

God's timing protects and prepares. If every dream came true instantly, wisdom and strength would never develop. Waiting seasons refine character and teach dependence on God, not just on outcomes.

Your life has its own seasons. Some friends may reach milestones before you. Some investments may seem to grow faster for others. Stay patient with your process. God's way often looks slow but ends up strong. Let patience do its work.

Practicing Patience

Staying patient is much more than waiting in silence. Patience means staying faithful in the small things, day after day. Keep saving what you can, keep giving with a cheerful heart, and keep learning, even if progress feels slow. Growth does not always show up right away, but every wise habit you practice lays another brick in your foundation.

Avoid the trap of measuring your life by someone else's timeline. Comparison can steal your peace. Your harvest is on its own schedule. Focus on your next step, not someone else's results. Remember, "he who gathers by labor will increase" (Proverbs 13:11, NKJV). This is your process, honor it.

Small wins are worth celebrating. Did you save a little more this month? Did you resist an impulse to spend or give generously even when it stretched you? Thank God for these milestones. They are signs that your seed is working, even if the field still looks bare.

Patience is active. Use waiting seasons to pray and prepare. Ask God for wisdom about what's ahead. Organize your finances, clear clutter, finish a course, or make space for what you hope to receive. This shows faith that a harvest is on the way.

Keep a simple journal or note on your phone. Record what you're sowing, your time, effort, or money. Write down every breakthrough, even the small ones. Over time, you will see patterns of faithfulness and blessing.

What have you been waiting for? How can you keep hope alive while you wait? Maybe it's a job, a house, a financial goal, or healing in a relationship. Remind yourself: God is never late. Your patience is proof of your faith. The best harvests take time, and what you're building will be worth the wait.

21

THE LAW OF RISK MANAGEMENT: PROTECTING WHAT YOU'RE BUILDING

"A prudent man foresees evil and hides himself, but the simple pass on and are punished."— *Proverbs 22:3 (NKJV)*

Is it faith to ignore danger? Or is wisdom a partner to faith? Many people believe that trusting God means never planning for the unexpected. Yet scripture teaches that wise preparation honors God and protects His blessing in your life. The Law of Risk Management says: Faith prepares, not panics. True wisdom means protecting what God gives you, faith is not recklessness.

God calls you to walk in faith, but not in denial. Preparation and prayer work together. Just as you would lock your door at night or fasten your seatbelt, risk management is simply about honoring God through stewardship, being a faithful caretaker, not a careless gambler. He has entrusted you with resources, relationships, and opportunities. Planning for trouble is not a lack of faith; it is wisdom in action.

Risk management touches every part of life. This includes having emergency savings, thinking ahead about your business or job, and making sure your family is secure if something unexpected happens. It can also mean setting boundaries in relationships or making backup plans at work. Simple actions, like buying insurance or having written agreements, are not signs of fear but acts of wise protection.

Scripture makes it clear: wise people anticipate trouble and act before it arrives, while the foolish live as if nothing bad could ever happen. Proverbs 22:3 paints this picture so plainly. Ecclesiastes 11:2 urges you not to depend on just one option, but to spread out your efforts, because the future holds many unknowns.

Real faith does not ignore reality. Godly wisdom looks ahead, listens for warning signs, and takes simple, practical steps to avoid loss. When you steward what God gives, you make room for more blessing and protect the fruit of your hard work. Wise risk management is how you honor God and secure your increase for generations to come.

Risk Management in the Bible and Today

Think about the difference between someone who prepares and someone who simply hopes for the best. Preparation is not just a good habit, it is a theme woven through scripture, proven in the lives of the wise. Risk management means you protect what matters, not out of fear, but out of faith and stewardship.

Noah's Ark stands as one of the most powerful biblical pictures of this principle. God spoke to Noah about a coming flood, and Noah responded not with panic, but with obedience and foresight. For years, he built the ark, gathering supplies and following every instruction. People around him laughed, but Noah's preparation saved his family and kept God's promise alive for future generations. His actions show that true faith leads to wise, often unpopular, preparation.

Joseph's story in Genesis 41 highlights another side of godly risk management. Pharaoh's dream warned of a coming famine after years of abundance. Joseph, trusting God's wisdom, advised Pharaoh to store grain during the good years. When the famine hit, Egypt was ready, not only able to survive but able to bless others. Joseph's practical plan saved a nation and his own family. He did not just trust God for a miracle; he put a strategy in place because God had revealed what was coming.

Proverbs 22:3 reminds us that wise people act on what they see coming, while those who ignore warning signs suffer the consequences. Ecclesiastes 11:2 encourages you to diversify and not rely on one stream, because the future holds unknown challenges.

Risk management shows up in ordinary life, too. Setting aside emergency savings means you can face a car repair or hospital bill without falling apart. Buying basic insurance, health, home, or business, protects your family or your small business from disaster. Having contracts in place, even with friends, guards against misunderstandings. Backing up important files saves precious memories or work from loss. Even maintaining a circle of trusted friends or mentors can help you weather personal storms.

A family with a small emergency fund finds peace when the refrigerator breaks. A local business owner avoids crisis by getting business insurance before opening their doors. A church with a financial reserve keeps the lights on during lean times. These stories play out every day, not out of anxiety, but out of respect for what God has provided.

Preparation is an act of faith. God expects you to pray, then act. He gives wisdom so you can protect and multiply His blessings. Simple habits, saving, insuring, planning, asking for advice, help you honor God's provision and keep your future secure. Wise risk management is not a lack of trust. It is how faith moves forward.

Simple Steps to Protect What You Build

Every wise builder puts safeguards in place long before a storm hits. The same is true for your life, finances, and purpose. Even small steps can make a lasting difference.

Start with an emergency fund. Decide on a fixed amount to set aside from each paycheck, even if it is only a few coins or dollars. Consistency is key. This habit creates a safety net for life's surprises, like medical bills or a job loss.

Diversify your income. Depending on a single job or business is risky. Use your talents to add a side stream, tutoring, crafting, digital work, or any skill that brings in a little extra. Each new stream brings more security and peace of mind.

Get insured if possible. Basic health, home, or business insurance shields you from losses that could wipe out years of progress. Insurance is not just for the wealthy; it is a wise tool for everyone.

Put things in writing. Contracts and clear agreements protect relationships and investments. Whether you are renting, lending, or going into business, written records keep everyone accountable and avoid confusion.

Prepare spiritually. Pray for wisdom before big decisions. Seek counsel from trusted mentors or church leaders. God often sends help through the voices of others, so stay open to advice.

Stay alert. Set a regular time each month to review your finances, check up on your plans, and assess your relationships. Catch problems early, and fix what needs fixing before small cracks become large gaps.

> What is one area of your life, money, work, health, or relationships, where you could put a new safety net in place this month?

God wants you to blend faith and wisdom in everything. Protecting what He gives honors the blessing and builds a legacy that lasts for you and your loved ones. Even the simplest act of preparation is a step toward lasting peace and prosperity.

22

❧

THE LAW OF ADAPTABILITY: PIVOTING FOR PROFIT AND PURPOSE

"I have learned both to be full and to be hungry, both to abound and to suffer need. I can do all things through Christ who strengthens me."— Philippians 4:12–13 (NKJV)

Thriving in a changing world does not depend on strength or intelligence alone. Those who rise above challenges have learned to adapt when life takes a turn. Adapting is not about surrendering your values or losing yourself. It is about shifting your approach, learning new skills, and moving forward with faith, even when the path ahead is different than expected.

Have you ever found yourself facing a sudden change, maybe a lost job, a big move, or a crisis in your family? In those moments, some freeze or give up, while others find ways to grow and even flourish. The secret is adaptability. When you are willing to adjust your plans and keep learning, setbacks turn into setups for something better.

Paul's words in Philippians give us a blueprint for resilience. He describes learning how to handle every season: abundance or lack, comfort, or difficulty. His strength did not come from circumstances. He rooted his confidence in Christ, who empowered him to handle anything.

Adaptability is not a personality trait you are born with. It is a spiritual and practical skill that can be cultivated, one step at a time. You build it every time you face a new problem with an open mind and a willing heart. Instead of clinging to what no longer works, you ask, "What can I learn? How can I move forward from here?"

No one can predict what tomorrow will bring. Change comes to every life, often when you least expect it. Adaptability means you do not have to fear those changes. You are equipped to handle them, growing stronger, wiser, and more confident each time you trust God and take a step into the new.

Every season of life offers a chance to practice this law. You are not stuck. You are not powerless. God gives you everything you need to adjust and thrive, no matter what changes around you. Even small steps of adaptability can open new doors and bring peace in uncertain times.

Adaptability in the Bible and Real Life

Adaptability stands out most when the comfortable path suddenly closes. In the darkest famine described in 2 Kings 7, four lepers sat at the city gate. Their options were bleak, stay put and die, enter the city, and perish, or try the enemy's camp. The familiar doors had shut. With nothing left to lose, they made a choice to move forward, even though it meant walking into the unknown. As they arrived at the camp, they discovered that God had already cleared the way. The enemy had fled. Food and supplies waited for those willing to take the risk. Their decision to act, to adapt, unlocked breakthrough not only for themselves but for an entire city.

Staying stuck can feel safe, but it only guarantees more of the same. Adaptability means you look for what God might be doing next, even when you feel afraid or uncertain. Sometimes the miracle is already waiting; it just takes one small step out of old routines.

Paul's testimony in Philippians 4 gives us another picture of adaptability. He wrote, *"I know how to be abased, and I know how to abound... I can do all things through Christ who strengthens me."* Paul faced prison, hunger, shipwreck, and rejection. He learned to adjust his attitude and habits in every season, never blaming circumstances for his peace. His flexibility came from his trust in Christ, not from perfect conditions. No matter what changed around him, he believed God could strengthen him for anything.

You see adaptability every day, not just in Bible stories, but in real life. A worker loses his job at a factory and decides to learn computer skills online. He starts small, faces setbacks, but over time lands a new role he never thought possible. A local baker watches sales drop, then uses social media and home delivery to keep her business alive and even attract new customers. Families that face sickness or a move band together, talk openly about the changes, and find creative ways to support each other.

What do these stories have in common? They show that those who adapt do not pretend everything is fine. They grieve losses, accept reality, and then ask, "What's my next move?" Growth starts with a willingness to learn new things and a heart open to feedback and help from others.

• Willingness to learn a new skill or try a new path

• Openness to honest advice and encouragement

• Trust that God brings good even when change feels painful

Change does not equal failure. It is an invitation. Each new season, whether forced by crisis or chosen in faith, holds opportunities you might never see if you refuse to move. Adaptability is not about doing it all on your own. It is about trusting God, welcoming help, and moving forward, one step at a time.

How to Practice Adaptability

Adaptability grows strongest through simple, daily choices. You do not need to overhaul your entire life to become more flexible, just start where you are with practical steps.

Be a learner. Pick up a book, watch a tutorial, or ask someone you trust for advice. Treat every change or setback as a classroom. What can you discover about yourself or your world that you didn't know before?

Stay flexible. Hold your plans with an open hand. When something blocks your way, pause, and try another approach instead of quitting. Adaptable people see detours as possibilities, not roadblocks.

Ask for help. No one is meant to adapt alone. Reach out to a friend, mentor, or professional when you need guidance. Honest conversations can reveal options you had not considered.

Find God in the change.

Prayer opens your eyes to opportunities even in unwanted transitions. Ask, "Lord, what are You teaching me in this season?" Trust that He will show you something valuable in every situation.

Take small steps. If you feel overwhelmed, break down change into one manageable action at a time. Adjust your routine, try a new way to solve a problem, or simply reach out for support. Every shift forward counts.

Celebrate growth. Look back at moments when you felt stuck and notice the ways God brought you through. Thank Him for new strengths, deeper relationships, or skills you gained along the way.

Reflect for a moment: What is one area of your life where you feel stuck? What is one small change or step you could take this week to move forward?

You really can do all things through Christ who strengthens you. Adaptability is not just survival, it is thriving, no matter what season you are in. With God's help, every change holds a hidden invitation to grow.

23

THE LAW OF NETWORKING: WEALTH THROUGH RELATIONSHIPS

"He who walks with wise men will be wise, but the companion of fools will be destroyed."— *Proverbs 13:20 (NKJV)*

Who you know, and who knows you, can open doors that skills or money alone cannot. **Your networking is your net worth.** Relationships are a form of wealth. **As the saying goes, "networking is your net worth."** The right connection at the right moment can move you further in a week than you could in a year on your own.

Think about it for a moment: Have you ever landed a job, gained a valuable client, or received an unexpected blessing simply because someone remembered you, introduced you, or spoke up on your behalf? Most people find that their biggest breakthroughs came through a person, not just their own efforts.

In God's Kingdom, relationships are part of His design for blessing and progress. No one is meant to build wealth, influence, or a meaningful life alone. From the start, God said, *"It is not good that man should be alone"* (Genesis 2:18). That truth goes far beyond marriage, it is about every area of life. Support, encouragement, wisdom, and even protection often flow through our connections.

Networking sometimes gets a bad reputation as a "business trick" or a way to use people for personal gain. True networking is not about collecting business cards or making shallow connections. It is about building genuine, two-way relationships rooted in trust and respect. When you care about others' growth, open doors for them, and stay loyal through ups and downs, you create a web of blessing that God can use to elevate you both.

You do not need a big personality or a huge network to start. A small circle of wise, encouraging, and resourceful people is worth more than a crowd of shallow contacts. Focus on quality over quantity. Walk with the wise, learn from their experience, and let your life become richer because of the people God brings your way.

Networking is a spiritual principle as much as a practical one. You honor God when you seek out good company, invest in others, and let others invest in you. **Your relationships often determine your reach, your influence, and your increase.** Walking with the wise will make you wise, and strong relationships can become one of your greatest assets in every season.

Networking in the Bible and Real Life

Who you walk with today can shape the direction of your life tomorrow. The Bible is filled with stories where a single relationship changed someone's destiny. One powerful example is **Naaman in 2 Kings 5**. Naaman was a respected military commander, yet he suffered from leprosy. His breakthrough did not come from his rank or wealth, but from a young servant girl who spoke up and pointed him to the prophet Elisha. **One connection changed everything.** Through obedience and the right guidance, Naaman received healing and restoration. His story shows that God often uses relationships, even unexpected ones, as the pathway to miracles.

Think about Ruth and Naomi. After losing her husband, Ruth clung to Naomi, refusing to let hardship break their bond. This loyalty put Ruth in position to meet Boaz. One relationship opened the door to provision, a new family, and a legacy that reached all the way to King David, and ultimately to Jesus. Ruth's story shows that kindness, loyalty, and being present for others can completely rewrite your story. A single connection can make all the difference.

You do not have to look far to find similar stories today. Many people find their first job through a recommendation. Businesses grow through referrals. Opportunities often come through mentors, friends, church members, or colleagues. These everyday moments reveal a deeper truth: **connections create opportunities.**

Healthy relationships deliver more than opportunities. They bring wisdom you might not find on your own, encouragement when you want to give up, and new options when doors seem closed. People you know, family, teachers, pastors, colleagues, often see gifts in you before you do. They can help you avoid mistakes and cheer you forward, especially when you doubt yourself.

Everyone can build meaningful connections, even if you are shy or have a small circle. You do not need to collect hundreds of names or become the center of attention. What matters is authenticity: reaching out, offering help, staying loyal, and being open to receive from others. Focus on serving before seeking favors. Take time to ask questions and listen. Thank people who help you. Small gestures build strong bridges.

Key reminders for building strong connections:

- Reach out to those around you, family, friends, church, work, or community.

- Be genuinely curious and caring about others' stories and needs.

- Support others first; look for ways to serve before you ask for help.

- Follow up and express gratitude, kindness keeps relationships healthy.

- Stay authentic; real relationships outlast shallow networking.

Meaningful relationships are not reserved for a select few. They are available to anyone willing to invest kindness, humility, and time. God can use even one relationship to open a door, spark a dream, or carry you through a hard season. Networking, at its heart, is about loving people well, and letting others love and help you, too.

Practical Steps for Everyone on How to Network

You do not need to be outgoing or have a big social circle to build powerful connections. Every relationship starts with one simple step. Reach out to someone you already know, family, friends, church members, or colleagues. Ask for advice or an introduction if you need it. Many people want to help but do not know you are looking unless you speak up.

Focus on giving before you ask for anything. Help, encourage, or support others wherever you can. Offer to listen, share a resource, or simply check in on someone. Serving first builds trust and opens hearts. Networking built on giving, not just getting, creates relationships that last.

Curiosity is a secret advantage. Ask real questions and listen closely. People remember those who genuinely care about their stories. You do not need all the answers, just an open heart and attentive ears. When you show real interest, doors open naturally.

Follow up and stay connected, even when you are not looking for something. Send a note, text, or call to say hello, check in, or offer encouragement. Little gestures mean a lot and remind people that you value them beyond what they can do for you.

Express gratitude often. Thank people for advice, introductions, or support. Gratitude deepens connections and keeps relationships healthy. A thankful spirit stands out in a world of hurry.

Most importantly, stay authentic. Be yourself, not a version you think others want. Real relationships are built on honesty, kindness, and respect, not on impressing others or chasing approval. When you walk with authenticity, you attract connections that fit your life and values.

> Who is one person you can reconnect with or encourage this week? What is one way you can serve someone in your network? Take that step today.

Your next breakthrough, idea, or opportunity could be just one relationship away. Walk with the wise, invest in others, and watch God use your connections for lasting good.

24

THE LAW OF CONTINUOUS LEARNING: STAYING SHARP TO STAY RELEVANT

"Wisdom is the principal thing; Therefore, get wisdom. And in all your getting, get understanding." — Proverbs 4:7 (NKJV)

When was the last time you learned something new? Think about how much could change if you picked up a fresh skill or gained a new insight this week. Some of the biggest breakthroughs in life and work happen because someone chose to learn again, even after school was long behind them.

The Law of Continuous Learning is simple: *Those who keep learning keep growing, your mind, skills, and opportunities multiply when you never stop seeking knowledge.* God's plan for you is not a life of getting stuck or stale, but one of growth, physically, spiritually, and mentally. Growth is not a one-time event. Each season of life calls for new wisdom, and each step forward demands more understanding.

Learning is not limited to a classroom or a certain age. School may finish, but your education never ends. The most successful and fulfilled people develop the habit of staying curious and hungry for new knowledge, whether they are sixteen or sixty. When you keep learning, you prepare yourself for the next assignment God has for you. Stagnation brings frustration and regret, but fresh wisdom opens doors you never saw before.

Many miss out on new levels of blessing because they assume they already know enough or think they are too old to start again. The world changes. Opportunities shift. God gives fresh instructions. Those who stay teachable move forward, while those who stop learning fall behind, no matter how smart or gifted they once were.

You have access to more knowledge than any generation before you. Books, courses, mentors, and free resources are everywhere. Start where you are. Learning is not about being the smartest in the room, it is about being willing to grow and apply new understanding. The next step in your destiny could be tied to the next thing you learn.

Learning is for everyone, every age, every stage, every season. When you make learning a habit, you step into God's ongoing promotion and protection. Stay teachable, and you will keep rising.

Continuous Learning in the Bible and Real Life

Think about the difference one new idea or skill can make in a person's life. Scripture is full of men and women whose progress depended not just on what they already knew, but on their willingness to seek wisdom, ask questions, and grow every step of the way.

Solomon, known as the wisest man who ever lived, asked God for wisdom above anything else. He understood the value of learning so deeply that he wrote, *"Wisdom is the principal thing; Therefore, get wisdom. And in all your getting, get understanding"* (Proverbs 4:7 NKJV). He knew that riches, influence, and favor all follow those who make wisdom their priority.

Look at the boy Jesus in the temple (Luke 2:46–52). His parents found Him sitting with the teachers, listening, and asking questions. Even as the Son of God, Jesus valued learning. Scripture says He increased in wisdom and stature and found favor with God and men. Growth did not come by default, it came through curiosity, listening, and a desire to learn from others.

Daniel and Joseph also stand out as examples. Daniel and his friends learned the language and literature of Babylon, gaining knowledge and skills that set them apart and led to promotion. Joseph's willingness to learn new ways, first as a servant, then as a leader in Egypt, brought solutions that saved nations and elevated him to authority. Both men were favored because they continued to grow, learn, and adapt, regardless of circumstances.

This principle still applies today. *A young employee who signs up for free online courses at work begins to gain skills others overlook. Promotions come, not just because of hard work, but because of the habit of learning.* A mother at home starts watching online tutorials, learns digital marketing, and is soon running a small business that helps provide for her family. A retired grandfather discovers local workshops at the library, stays sharp, and finds fresh purpose through mentoring young people.

Learning opens doors. It unlocks creativity, gives you confidence to try new things, and helps you adapt when life shifts. The person who never stops learning becomes valuable in any setting, at work, at home, in church, or in the community.

Many regrets missed opportunities because they stopped growing. Those who keep learning, even one step at a time, prepare themselves for the next assignment God has for them. *Opportunities come to those who are ready, and readiness comes from learning.* God honors a teachable spirit, at any age.

The path of continuous learning does not mean rushing to get a degree or cramming facts. It means being open, curious, and humble enough to ask, listen, and apply new knowledge. Each season of life brings fresh lessons and possibilities. The door to your next breakthrough may be waiting on the other side of the next thing you decide to learn.

How to Become a Lifelong Learner

Learning is not reserved for a special few. You have everything you need to grow, right where you are. Here are a few ways to make learning a natural, enjoyable part of your life:

Read Regularly. Start with the Bible, God's wisdom for every season. Pick up books that feed your faith, help you with money, work, parenting, or a skill you want to master. Even a few pages a day can shift your thinking and open new possibilities.

Take Courses. Search for free or low-cost classes online or in your community. Libraries, churches, and local groups often offer workshops or talks. One class a year can make a bigger impact than you might expect.

Find a Mentor. There is always someone who has gone further in a certain area. Ask questions, listen to their advice, and try out what you learn. Mentors help you avoid mistakes and make faster progress.

Ask Questions. Do not let pride keep you from learning. If you do not know something, ask. Curiosity is a sign of wisdom, not weakness.

Join a Learning Community. Growth multiplies when you learn with others. Get involved in a Bible study, a book club, or an online forum. Share what you learn and encourage each other to keep going.

Take a moment and reflect: What is one area you want to grow in this year? Is there a book, course, or mentor that could help you move forward?

No matter your age, background, or starting point, you are never too late to learn. Wisdom is a lifelong pursuit. As you choose to keep learning, you prepare yourself for God's best, opening doors for blessings you may not even see yet. Stay teachable, and let each new step carry you closer to the life God has for you.

25

The Law of Alignment: Positioning Yourself for Increase

"He shall be like a tree planted by the rivers of water, that brings forth its fruit in its season... and whatever he does shall prosper."
— *Psalm 1:3 (NKJV)*

Do you ever feel like you're working hard, but not really moving forward? Many people hustle day after day, only to find that all their sweat leads them in circles instead of toward real growth. Often, the issue is not a lack of effort or even talent, it's misalignment.

The Law of Alignment says that your greatest progress comes when your values, decisions, and resources all point in the same direction. When every part of your life, what you believe, what you do, and how you spend, lines up with God's assignment for you, new clarity and fruitfulness will follow. The difference between scattered effort and focused progress is alignment.

Picture a tree planted by water, its roots deep and its leaves always green. It flourishes no matter the weather because its life is connected to the right source.

The psalmist calls this person "blessed." Why? Not because they work more than everyone else, but because they keep their roots in the right place. They avoid unhealthy influences, meditate on God's Word, and allow His wisdom to shape their path. The result is a stable, fruitful life that prospers in every season.

Alignment means being honest about your habits and priorities. Are your daily choices bringing you closer to your God-given purpose, or pulling you in a hundred directions? Are your spending and relationships supporting your calling, or just filling space? True prosperity is not just about having more things, it's about being planted, nourished, and fruitful in the right things.

This law is not just a spiritual concept. Alignment is practical. When your goals, actions, and money all point north, toward what God has put in your heart, you save time, reduce stress, and multiply your results. Clarity brings peace. Alignment brings progress.

Start with honest reflection. Ask God for wisdom to see where things are out of line. When you adjust your life to match His design, you unlock the supernatural promise of Psalm 1: whatever you do will prosper, because you are rooted where you belong.

Alignment in Scripture and Everyday Life

What would your life look like if your choices and your values all moved in the same direction? When you hear stories of people who seem unshakable, full of purpose and contentment, often it comes down to one thing: alignment. Their roots are deep, their priorities are clear, and their actions reflect what matters most.

Psalm 1:1–3 paints the picture of this kind of person. The blessed life starts with a simple practice, choosing influences and company with care. Instead of drifting with whatever is popular, the person who flourishes meditates on God's Word and allows it to shape every decision. When the storms come, they stand firm.

Their life bears fruit at the right time, and whatever they do prospers, because their foundation is stable.

Jesus gives us the ultimate example of alignment. Throughout His ministry, He spoke openly about doing only what He saw His Father doing (John 5:19). He did not waste energy chasing every request or opportunity. Every step, every word, every act of compassion flowed from being deeply connected to God's will. His life models focus and fruitfulness, not busyness.

Alignment is not just a spiritual ideal. It shows up in everyday life in very practical ways:

- A single parent who decides that every spending decision will reflect their values, so they set aside part of each paycheck for giving, another part for savings, and carefully plan the rest to meet the family's true needs. This alignment brings peace, even if the income is modest.

- A business owner who turns down a tempting but questionable contract, choosing instead to pursue projects that reflect integrity. Over time, this creates a reputation of trust, and the right opportunities begin to find them.

- A family sits together at the kitchen table, talking about their hopes for the year. They write down goals for learning, health, generosity, and fun, then check in every month to see how everyone is doing. When everyone's heading in the same direction, energy multiplies, and progress feels easier.

When life feels scattered or off track, alignment may be the missing piece. Misalignment, when your words say one thing, but your habits point another way, creates anxiety, confusion, and wasted effort. When your goals, habits, and spending are in sync, clarity replaces chaos. Even small adjustments bring big results.

- Alignment is not about perfection. It is about being intentional.

- Honest self-checks matter more than big, dramatic changes.

- God honors every effort to realign with His purpose, no matter where you start.

Pause and ask: What is one area where you feel out of sync? A small change, one daily habit, one new boundary, one honest conversation, can start to realign your life, bringing you closer to the stable, fruitful blessing described in Psalm 1.

Practical Checklists and Steps to Realign

If you sense a gap between your intentions and your results, it's time to pause and realign. Change starts with honest reflection and one small step at a time. Use this simple checklist to bring your life, habits, and money into agreement with your God-given purpose.

Review Your Values

Write down your top five priorities. What do you believe God wants you to focus on? These might include faith, family, health, generosity, or growth. Seeing your values in writing brings instant clarity.

Check Your Goals

Ask yourself if your current goals reflect those values. Are you chasing what truly matters to you, or trying to impress others? Adjust your focus to line up with your real purpose, not just what looks good on paper.

Audit Your Actions

Take a quick look at your calendar and your bank statement. Where do your time and money go each week? If your habits point away from your values, you have an opportunity, not a failure. Even one small change can start a new direction.

Adjust Your Habits

Pick one area, budget, schedule, commitments, or relationships, and make a practical change. Cancel an unnecessary subscription, carve out time for prayer, or limit activities that drain your energy.

Pray for Guidance

Ask God to reveal any hidden misalignment and to strengthen your resolve. Pray for courage to say yes to what matters and no to distractions.

Get Accountability

Share your realignment plan with a trusted friend or group. Invite encouragement, feedback, and gentle reminders. You do not have to do this alone.

> Where do you sense the need for realignment? What is one small action you can take this week to move closer to God's purpose for you?

God's promise stands: when you are rooted in Him and walk in His ways, you will flourish in every season. Alignment brings lasting fruit, peace, and progress, no matter where you start.

26

The Law of Prophetic Alignment: Partnering with Heaven's Blueprint

"He who receives a prophet in the name of a prophet shall receive a prophet's reward..."— *Matthew 10:41 (NKJV)*

Have you ever sensed God prompting you to do something unexpected, only to watch things shift in your life in ways you never planned? These moments of divine direction are at the heart of prophetic alignment. Sometimes a single word or instruction from God changes the entire course of your finances, family, or future. This law is about learning to listen, trust, and act when God speaks, whether through Scripture, a trusted voice, or a quiet nudge from the Holy Spirit.

Prophetic alignment means recognizing when God is speaking about your season and choosing to obey, even if it challenges your comfort or logic. In 2 Kings 4, a widow faced hopeless debt. Through Elisha, God gave a clear and unusual instruction: borrow empty vessels and pour out her last oil. She followed through, and her little became more than enough. God's word turned her scarcity into overflow.

This law does not belong to a select group of spiritual experts. Jesus made it clear, anyone who welcomes a true prophetic word can access the blessing attached to it. God is eager to guide every believer. The breakthrough you long for may come through a prompt you did not expect.

Prophetic alignment is not mystical or strange. It is practical, timely direction that fits with God's character and always lines up with His Word. Sometimes it comes as a whisper in prayer, a verse that leaps off the page, or wise counsel from someone who loves God.

When you learn to recognize and respond to these God-given instructions, you open doors to provision, ideas, and opportunities that you could not produce in your own strength. Breakthrough is often one act of obedience away. This law reminds you to stay attentive and willing, because God still speaks, and He delights to lead you into blessing.

Prophetic Alignment in the Bible and Today

When God speaks, circumstances shift. History is filled with moments where a single word from the Lord rewrote someone's future, especially in the area of provision and breakthrough. These are not fairy tales, but patterns that still apply to your life today.

In 2 Kings 4, a widow faces the threat of losing her sons to creditors. With nothing but a small jar of oil, she goes to Elisha, the prophet. His instruction is clear: borrow as many empty vessels as you can and pour your oil into them. She gathers the vessels, begins to pour, and the oil flows until every container is filled. When she returns to Elisha, he tells her, *"Go, sell the oil and pay your debt; and you and your sons live on the rest."* The crisis is reversed because she listens to God's word and acts on it. The word believed and obeyed multiplies her little into abundance.

A similar miracle unfolds in 2 Kings 7. Samaria is starving, surrounded by enemies, hope all but lost. Elisha announces, *"Tomorrow about this time, food will be sold cheaply at the gate of Samaria."* Skepticism is high, but God moves. Four lepers, desperate and outcast, step toward the enemy camp, only to find it deserted and overflowing with food and treasure. Their report saves the city. The prophecy becomes reality as soon as someone moves on God's instruction. The lesson is unmistakable: breakthrough often comes when you act on what God says, even when logic protests.

Jesus Himself points to the power of prophetic alignment in Matthew 10:40–42. He promises a "prophet's reward" to those who honor and receive God's messengers. This reward is not reserved for a spiritual elite, but available to anyone who is willing to discern, honor, and act on God's word in season.

Modern stories echo these ancient truths. A woman, nudged to give generously during a time of personal financial strain, soon finds doors open a job offer, a cancelled debt, or an unexpected gift. A business owner receives a strong sense in prayer to shift strategy or launch a new product, resulting in fresh growth. A family starts saving after feeling prompted in church, and when a medical bill arrives months later, they are prepared.

These stories share a common thread: each step of obedience starts with a word and ends with provision or rescue that only God could orchestrate.

Every prophetic word should align with God's heart and His Word. God does not contradict Himself, and He always builds your trust, not fear. Prophetic alignment is not about chasing signs or formulas; it is about tuning your heart to God, ready to respond when He leads.

Your story is not finished. God can speak a word in any season, through Scripture, a trusted mentor, or a quiet whisper, and set new provision in motion. When you honor what He says, you step into blessing designed just for you.

How to Receive, Believe, and Act on a Prophetic Word

God speaks in many ways, and His instructions can bring dramatic change, if you are ready to listen and act. Prophetic alignment is not reserved for a few "spiritual giants." It is a daily invitation to every believer who wants to honor God and unlock His provision. Here's how you can approach prophetic words wisely and faithfully.

Begin by positioning your heart. Create space for God by setting aside regular time in prayer and Scripture. Invite Him to speak, and let your heart be open to His guidance. You may find that in these quiet moments, God brings clarity to an issue or nudges you toward a next step.

Next, discern what you hear. Every true word from God will line up with the Bible and His loving character. Ask yourself, does this instruction bring peace, clarity, or repeated confirmation? Wise counsel from mature believers and a consistent inner prompting often provide confirmation. "*Test all things; hold fast what is good*" (1 Thessalonians 5:21, NKJV). The prophetic builds faith, not fear.

Receiving a prophetic instruction may sometimes stretch your comfort zone. God's ideas can feel bigger or riskier than you planned. Resist the urge to dismiss the word just because it is unfamiliar or challenges you. Faith begins when you say yes, even if your step feels small.

Act in obedience. Move forward as God leads, remembering that the miracle came for the widow only after she gathered the jars, and for the lepers only as they stepped out. God honors movement. If your action is humble and practical, even as simple as starting a savings habit, reaching out to someone, or sowing a seed, He can use it.

Stay humble and teachable throughout the process. If you mishear or things unfold differently than expected, treat it as a learning moment, not a defeat. If God moves, give Him all the glory. Balance is vital: you are not called to chase after prophecies, but to cultivate a life that is sensitive, discerning, and ready to respond.

Where might God be nudging you right now? What is one small step, financial, relational, or practical, that you could take in response? Take a moment to reflect, pray, and write it down.

> Remember, God's desire is to lead you into greater fruitfulness, and He cares about every detail, including your wealth.

Breakthrough does not begin with striving, but with hearing, trusting, and obeying. When you receive His word with faith and move in obedience, you align yourself for blessing and open doors that no one else could have planned.

CONCLUSION

You are not average. You are appointed for more than survival, more than daily hustle, more than making ends meet. You are a Kingdom builder, anointed to multiply, trusted to manage, and assigned to impact. You are God's answer to generational lack, financial bondage, and empty legacy. Your hands carry solutions. Your mind holds blueprints. Your spirit carries access.

You were born for this.

You are stepping into a new financial authority, not rooted in pride, but in purpose. Cycles of lack, delay, and fear are breaking off of you. You are not bound to your past patterns. You are not limited by what your parents did or did not give you. The Father is placing strategy in your heart and divine power in your hands.

You are a Joseph, rising in wisdom to manage divine resources. You are a Deborah, governing with clarity, courage, and counsel. You are a Daniel, wealthy in discernment and positioned to influence systems. You are a Proverbs 31 builder, productive, generous, and fearless about the future.

You will build. You will multiply. You will give and still have more. You will teach and still grow deeper. What God puts in your hands will not run dry.

> Speak this aloud:
> *"I am a Kingdom financier. I walk in wisdom, abundance, and purpose. My wealth is my worship, and my legacy is my testimony. I will not lack, I will lead."*

Your time is now. Your seed is ready. Your impact is just beginning.

You are more than a faithful steward. You are a financier of Kingdom purpose. You've been given the power to create wealth, not just to enjoy it, but to establish God's covenant in the earth. You are called to resource vision, fund ministry, rebuild broken systems, and release impact that echoes into eternity.

God has entrusted you with ideas, income, and influence. That trust comes with divine responsibility. Luke 8:3 tells us of women who funded Jesus' ministry. They didn't wait for someone else to sponsor the Gospel, they rose up and owned their assignment. Deuteronomy 8:18 reminds you that the ability to produce wealth is not talent, it is covenant power. And 2 Corinthians 9 declares that God enriches you in every way so you can abound in good works.

This is not about riches for show. This is about wealth on assignment.

Let the fear of ownership fall away. Let the false humility dissolve. You are not greedy for wealth; you are gripped by purpose. The world is groaning for people who walk in financial wisdom and spiritual fire. Be one of them.

Don't hide from this calling. Don't apologize for it. Own it. Rise up. Steward it well.

You were never called to smallness. Playing it safe, holding back, and shrinking to fit someone else's comfort will not fulfill your assignment. Abundance is not pride; it is alignment with God's covenant. When you walk in wisdom and overflow, you become a demonstration of His goodness.

Step boldly into this next season. Walk in faith without apology. Build with strategy, not hesitation. Give with conviction, not fear. God didn't raise you up just to be blessed, He raised you to become a blessing on assignment.

This is not about luxury. This is about legacy. Your increase carries impact. Your overflow becomes provision for someone else's answered prayer. You are stepping into a life where your obedience feeds nations, funds revival, and fuels generational change.

Don't shrink to fit religious boxes or cultural fears. You were made for overflow, not just so you can enjoy it, but so others can taste the goodness of God through you.

You are Heaven's builder, Earth's financier, and Hell's threat. Advance boldly, because what you carry funds revival, fuels legacy, and shifts history.

Go. Build. Multiply. Give. Teach. Transform.

Daily Affirmations

1. I am a millionaire.

2. I am my own and I am in the hands of Jesus.

3. I do business in the name of Jesus.

4. I prosper in the name of Jesus.

5. I am blessed coming in, and I am blessed, and I am blessed going out.

6. I am the head and not the tail.

7. I am above and not beneath.

8. The joy of the Lord is my strength.

9. The favor of God works for me.

10. There are no limits to my success.

11. My steps are ordered by God.

12. I walk in divine wisdom.

13. I do Kingdom business and earthly business with integrity.

14. Every element of my day shall cooperate with my purpose and destiny.

15. Anything or anyone assigned to undermine, frustrate, hinder, or hurt me, I command to be silenced, in the name of Jesus.

16. I greet today with great anticipation of the good things God has prepared for me.

17. I decree and declare that a new day is dawning for my business.

18. I download success, prosperity, wealth, vision, direction, ingenuity, creativity, and resourcefulness from Your Spirit into my business.

19. I believe and confess that God's abundance flows into my business.

20. I boldly command every hidden treasure of abundance to be exposed to me, that the riches of the ungodly will enter into my hand for favor and blessing.

21. I boldly command every drought and famine area in my business to be transformed into abundance, in the name of Jesus.

22. I confess that I have fresh excitement, a fresh mind, a fresh zeal and a fresh anointing that is uncontaminated and uncompromised, in the name of Jesus.

23. Increased productivity and profit is the lot of my business, in the name of Jesus.

24. My business is growing and expanding exponentially, in the name of Jesus.

25. My business grows in season and out of season.

26. Men and women bless me everywhere I go, in the name of Jesus.

27. I release my business from the clutches of financial hunger, in the name of Jesus.

28. I release angels to go and create favor for my business, in the name of Jesus.

29. God's plan is to elevate my business and not demote it.

30. I confess that I will be patient until my business is fully established, in the name of Jesus.

Adapted from JLS Ministries.

REFERENCE

Adeboye, E. A. (n.d.). *[Sermons and teachings]*.

Bible. (1982). *New King James Version*. ThomasNelson.

Bok, D. (n.d.). *If you think education is expensive, try ignorance.*

Buffett, W. (n.d.). *Never depend on a single income...*

Cicero. (n.d.). *[Quoted statement on gratitude]*.

Cole, E. L. (n.d.). *[Teachings and leadership statements]*.

Dyer, W. (2009). *Excuses begone!: How to change lifelong, self-defeating thinking habits.* Hay House.

Emmons, R. A., & Stern, R. (2013). Gratitude as a psychotherapeutic intervention. *Journal of Clinical Psychology, 69*(8),846–855.

Forbes Media. (2023). *America's richest families.*

Harvard University, Opportunity Insights. (2018). *TheOpportunity Atlas.*

Jaffe, C. A. (n.d.). *It's not your salary that makes you rich...*

Kaplan, H. (2010). Who wants to be a millionaire? Not the lottery winners. *Journal of Gambling Studies, 26*(4), 607–611.

Kiyosaki, R. T. (1997). *Rich dad poor dad.* WarnerBooks.

Lewis, C. S. (1942). *The Screw tape letters.* Geoffrey Bles.

Malcolm X. (1965). *Malcolm X speaks.* Grove Press.

Mandela, N. (1994). *Long walk to freedom.* Little,Brown and Company.

Munroe, M. (n.d.). *When purpose is not known, abuse is inevitable.*

Pew Research Center. (2023). *Financial literacy in theUnited States.*

Rand, A. (1957). *Atlas shrugged.* Random House.

Ramsey, D. (n.d.). *[Financial teachings and principles].*

Robbins, T. (1991). *Awaken the giant within.* FreePress.

Rohn, J. (n.d.). *You don't get paid for the hour...*

Thatcher, M. (n.d.). *[Public remarks on the GoodSamaritan].*

UNESCO. (2017). *Literacy rates and educational outcomes worldwide.*

U.S. Federal Reserve. (2023). *Report on the economic well-being of U.S. households.*

Wayne, D. (Dyer, W.). (n.d.). *Abundance is not something we acquire...*